Keeping Good People

Strategies

for Solving the

Dilemma

of the Decade

Roger E. Herman

McGraw-Hill, Inc.
New York   St. Louis   San Francisco   Auckland   Bogotá
Caracas   Hamburg   Lisbon   London   Madrid
Mexico   Milan   Montreal   New Delhi   Paris
San Juan   São Paulo   Singapore
Sydney   Tokyo   Toronto

2 3 4 5 6 7 8 9 0   DOC/DOC   9 7 6 5 4 3 2 1

ISBN 0-07-028369-9

Printed and bound by R. R. Donnelley & Sons Company.

Other books by Roger E. Herman

The Process of Excelling

Disaster Planning for Local Government

Emergency Operations Plan

Dedication

This book is dedicated to my parents, Carlton and Estelle Herman, who gave me the foundation to be a high achiever. They led by example and kept me alert and fighting with their constuctive criticism and encouragement.

It is dedicated to my wife, Sandy, who by her steadiness balances the ups and downs that occur in the life of a writer, professional speaker, and entrepreneur. I have been strengthened immeasurably by her optimism and intuition.

I also dedicate this book to a valued mentor who modestly disclaims any influence over my achievement. Charles M. King has served as a positive inspiration and motivation for me since we first met in 1974. God has blessed him as he has overcome a variety of challenges; his service to mankind is a beautiful example of what can be accomplished when one man gives of himself to help others succeed.

Acknowledgments

This page is the most difficult to write. While I have the opportunity here to thank those who contributed directly to this book, there is also an obligation to thank those who contributed indirectly to its development. No matter how hard an author may try to recognize everyone who helped make a dream become reality, there is always the risk of forgetting a number of people who deserve a salute.

With that risk in mind, I'll start by offering a special thank you to Anneliese Dilworth and Don Winton. These fellow consultants contributed directly to the design, the focus, and the text. Their involvement and sharing of their expertise strengthened this book.

Acknowledgment is a weak word to express my love and appreciation to my wife, Sandy, and our children. They have been both patient and encouraging through the seemingly endless nights and week-ends as this book was created. Their support is my source of energy and inspiration.

My team-mate at Herman Associates, Julie Jenewein, helped make this project a success in ways she doesn't even realize. Thanks for the years of trying new strategies, sometimes more frequently than appropriate. We keep learning.

And, finally, thanks to Marty James, and all our clients, friends, and fellow travellers who have strengthened my understanding, insight, and dedication over many years of learning, growth, practice, and service.

Table of Contents

Dedication
Acknowledgements
Preface *xv*
Introduction *xix*

Section One

1. **Good People and Their Value in Organizations** 3
2. **The Predicament** 7
3. **The Competitive Environment** 21
4. **What Good People Want** 37

Section Two

5. **Strategic Responses** 51

6. **Environmental Strategies** 57

    Strategy 6.1: Share a common vision.
    Strategy 6.2: Value each individual.
    Strategy 6.3: Work together as a team.
    Strategy 6.4: Loyalty is a two-way relationship.
    Strategy 6.5: Enthusiasm is justified and appropriate.
    Strategy 6.6: We are all here for the customer.
    Strategy 6.7: Have a set of Guiding Principles.
    Strategy 6.8: Offer stability, security, risk as needed.
    Strategy 6.9: Prohibit discrimination of any kind.
    Strategy 6.10: Eschew profanity.
    Strategy 6.11: Be fair and honest.
    Strategy 6.12: Facilitate a family feeling.
    Strategy 6.13: Value professional standing.
    Strategy 6.14: Promote integrity.
    Strategy 6.15: Encourage camaraderie.
    Strategy 6.16: Promote a healthy working environment.
    Strategy 6:17: Insist on workplace safety.

Strategy 6.18: Avoid stupid rules.
Strategy 6.19: Provide flexibility in working hours.
Strategy 6.20: Apply progressive discipline fairly.
Strategy 6.21: Make work fun.
Strategy 6.22: Celebrate achievements, birthdays, etc.
Strategy 6.23: Don't tolerate, remove unsuitable people.
Strategy 6.24: Conduct exit interviews.
Strategy 6.25: Establish clear policies.
Strategy 6.26: Administer policies uniformly.
Strategy 6.27: Provide advancement opportunities, promote from within.
Strategy 6.28: Give permission to fail or succeed.
Strategy 6.29: Management Commitment: People are our most important resource.
Strategy 6.30: Share information.
Strategy 6.31: Value all your people.
Strategy 6.32: Respond to complaints with solutions.
Strategy 6.33: Use your business plan.
Strategy 6.34: Within safety constraints, permit refreshments at work stations.
Strategy 6.35: Offer freedom of choice: break times, dress, vacations.
Strategy 6.36: Choose employees carefully the first time.
Strategy 6.37: Locate your company in a suitable environment
Strategy 6.38: Encourage people to personalize their work areas.
Strategy 6.39: Eliminate reserved personal parking.
Strategy 6.40: Provide effective communications systems.
Strategy 6.41: Equip people to be productive.
Strategy 6.42: Provide for appropriate child care services.
Strategy 6.43: Maintain comfortable atmospheric conditions.
Strategy 6.44: Use color constructively in decoration.

Strategy 6.45: Provide a safe, secure environment.

7. Relationship Strategies 111

Strategy 7.1: Understand behavioral styles.
Strategy 7.2: Appreciate values and ethical standards.
Strategy 7.3: Resolve conflicts.
Strategy 7.4: Hold regular meetings of your team members.
Strategy 7.5: Call spontaneous meetings.
Strategy 7.6: Facilitate open communication.
Strategy 7.7: Stick up for your people.
Strategy 7.8: Give recognition strategically and deliberately.
Strategy 7.9: Recognize the "new woman."
Strategy 7.10: Recognize other "special employees."
Strategy 7.11: Be patient.
Strategy 7.12: Show respect for others.
Strategy 7.13: Give people freedom and flexibility.
Strategy 7.14: Trust your people.
Strategy 7.15: Show genuine, sincere appreciation.
Strategy 7.16: Listen.
Strategy 7.17: Let people be who they are.
Strategy 7.18: Find opportunities to talk with people.
Strategy 7.19: Balance praise and criticism.
Strategy 7.20: Build everyone's self esteem.
Strategy 7.21: Don't gossip.
Strategy 7.22: Look for positives, not negatives.
Strategy 7.23: Express confidence.
Strategy 7.24: Enable people to be together.
Strategy 7.25: Care about people as individuals.
Strategy 7.26: Be accessible.
Strategy 7.27: Have a sense of humor.
Strategy 7.28: Set an example.
Strategy 7.29: Show leadership at the top of your organization.
Strategy 7.30: Reduce stress. Keep anxiety to stay sharp.

Strategy 7.31: Don't question or second-guess people all the time.

Strategy 7.32: Be firm and fair.

8. Task-Focused Strategies   165

Strategy 8.1: Give people real things to do.

Strategy 8.2: Provide challenges.

Strategy 8.3: Fight frustration.

Strategy 8.4: Remove barriers to task accomplishment.

Strategy 8.5: Adjust jobs to fit strengths, abilities, and talents.

Strategy 8.6: Empower people to work as a team.

Strategy 8.7: Mickey Mouse should be fun, not fundamental.

Strategy 8.8: Keep the promises you make.

Strategy 8.9: Provide the resources to get the job done.

Strategy 8.10: Avoid rejection, raw criticism, humiliation.

Strategy 8.11: Encourage and welcome new ideas.

Strategy 8.12: Define responsibilities.

Strategy 8.13: Define accountabilities.

Strategy 8.14: Define authority.

Strategy 8.15: Encourage initiative.

Strategy 8.16: Inspire and enable creativity and innovation.

Strategy 8.17: Establish limits, parameters.

Strategy 8.18: Know what your people are doing.

Strategy 8.19: Respond when people ask for approval or guidance.

Strategy 8.20: Give clear direction.

Strategy 8.21: Get people involved.

Strategy 8.22: Reduce reporting requirements.

Strategy 8.23: Don't look over peoples' shoulders.

Strategy 8.24: Don't keep people overtime without previous notice.

Strategy 8.25: Appreciate routine work.

Strategy 8.26: Enter into performance contracts.

Strategy 8.27: Fight boredom.
Strategy 8.28: Design tasks to meet personal needs.
Strategy 8.29: Give people a break.
Strategy 8.30: Give specifics in performance feedback.

9. Compensation Strategies   201

Strategy 9.1: Present the full value of compensation.
Strategy 9.2: Provide linking incentive opportunities to
all employees.
Strategy 9.3   Link performance with rewards.
Strategy 9.4   Leverage the total cash compensation
package for maximum effectiveness.
Strategy 9.5   Design reward system for employee
involvement.
Strategy 9.6   Compensate high potential/low skill
employees with a skills-based system.
Strategy 9.7   Use flexible benefits in a changing
workforce.
Strategy 9.8   Consider ESOPs and employee stock
ownership.

10. People Growing Strategies   215

Strategy 10.1: Give people challenging responsibilities.
Strategy 10.2: Support formal education.
Strategy 10.3: Offer learning materials for personal
growth
Strategy 10.4: Connect with outside resources for
learning materials.
Strategy 10.5: Send people to outside seminars.
Strategy 10.6: Have learners pass their training along to
others.
Strategy 10.7: Help people grow into bigger jobs.
Strategy 10.8: Enable people to discover the wealth of
talents they have.
Strategy 10.9: Encourage intellectual growth.
Strategy 10.10: Assign special projects.
Strategy 10.11: Build competency deliberately.

Strategy 10.12: Provide incentives for growth.

Section Three

11. **Tactics for Implementing Strategies**   **235**
12. **Combining Strategic Approaches for Optimum Results**   **245**
13. **Focus on Each Individual's Needs**   **249**
14. **A Perspective on the Future**   **257**

Appendices
A. Behavioral Styles, Leadership Styles   **265**
B. Behavioral and Corporate Values   **273**
C. Self Esteem in the Corporate Environment   **279**

Index   **289**

Preface

Running a business, institution, non-profit organization, or local government agency is certainly different today from what it was a generation or two ago.

Resources are not as plentiful as they once were. When we gather the resources we need, we have to make more creative uses of them to maximize our return on investment. The risk of losing those resources, even though we thought we had them well in hand, hangs over us like a Damocles sword.

Success is described in many different ways. Each of us subscribes to our own formula of achievement and satisfaction. However we define it, success rarely comes easily. Accomplishment takes time and hard work. In order to get things done in our lives, we have to marshall the necessary resources and apply them well.

For most of us, success is not achieved alone. Sure, we like to think we were responsible for what we've done and what we've become. We are. We provide the impetus, the leadership, the inspiration, the drive to make things happen.

But, other people are part of our success. Other people play a number of motivating and supporting roles to enable us to make a difference. In our complex society, we have become significantly interdependent. Particularly in organizational settings. Everything we do is connected with things other people do.

I have worked in business organizations, interacting with other people in one way or another, since I was in the ninth grade back in the 1950s. I've learned a few things. I've discovered what works...and what doesn't work. I won't say I have all the answers. No one really does.

In this book, as in my work, I enjoy sharing the answers, the approaches, that I have found to be successful. Some of these ideas and techniques I have learned and practiced personally. Others have come to me through other people--directly, through observation, and from reading what they have written. We learn from each other.

As you read through the pages that follow, you will benefit from the knowledge and experience gained by Anneliese Dilworth, Don Winton, myself, and countless others who have shared with us over the years.

In my work as a corporate consultant, focusing on the application and development of human resources, I have found it quite helpful to raise issues, to ask questions, to get people thinking in ways they had not been thinking before. A great deal of organizational success results from people looking critically and/or creatively at their circumstances, then designing better ways to do things.

I don't claim to have any great secrets that will change the world. You can't turn to a certain page in this book, recite some incantation, and watch amazed as a flash of lightning reveals the secrets of the universe!

Keeping Good People, like my previous book, *The Process of Excelling*, is an extension of my life's work. Through these writings, I aim to stimulate your thinking. If your awareness is raised, if you can see things you hadn't seen before, if you can see familiar things differently, then you will have the power of insight.

I can but share perspectives, approaches, ideas. Their value rests in what you do with the knowledge you gain from reading these words. Hopefully, some of what you discover in this book will serve as an inspiration for you to take actions to make a difference for your organization and for your people.

Most of the men and women who read this book will be leaders and managers of various kinds of organizations. Those organizations will include for-profit businesses of all types, not-for-profit organizations and agencies, educational institutions, local governments, and associations. While the purpose and technology of these entities may be quite different, all share the need to produce the greatest possible return on their investment in human resources.

Our human resources, our people, are at once the most valuable, the most costly, and the most volatile of all the resources we use to accomplish the organization's work. We need good people to get things done. One of our biggest challenges is to attract, integrate, motivate, and keep good people.

"Good" can be defined any way you wish. For some, the descriptor will apply to someone's technical expertise. For others, it will refer to dedication, productivity, drive and determination, high achievement, creative capacity, experience, educational level, position in the industry or field, or any combination of these and other factors. I will leave the definition to you, based on what qualities are most important to accomplish your goals.

As you continue with your reading, please consider me as your personal consultant. I'll be talking directly with you. It will be like having someone right there in the same room with you, sharing ideas, raising issues, encouraging, pointing out problem areas for you to consider.

Reading through this book will be a "cafeteria" experience for you. Some of what is offered you will hungrily and eagerly consume. Other things may not be what you are looking for. You may already be doing some of the things suggested, or they simply may not fit in your situation. You pick and choose, cafeteria-style. If you find but one good idea that makes a significant difference for you, our investment in each other will have been worthwhile.

There is so much that needs to be done in this field, I know I've missed some things. It's a human foible and a frustration for writers and speakers. After you've delivered the message, you think of something else you could have said. Or you discover something you didn't know before; and it didn't get in the book or speech or seminar. We all continue to learn and grow, discovering things we didn't know before.

If you have some ideas that I haven't covered in this book, please let me know. If there are some techniques or approaches that have worked for you, I'd like to learn about them. If enough new ideas are gathered, a revision or sequel to this book is certainly appropriate. I promise you it will not be titled "Son of Keeping Good People" or "Keeping Good People, Part II."

So, read, learn, apply, and enjoy!

Roger E. Herman
19 North Main Street
Rittman, Ohio 44270-1407

Introduction

This book is written to be easily read and applied, as a guidebook for organizational leaders. It is designed so it can be read cover-to-cover, but also so it can be used as a reference book for ideas.

Attracting, recruiting, and keeping good people is becoming an increasingly critical challenge for us. No one person can have all the answers. In creating this book, which I hope will help you find some new answers for yourself, I have talked with a great number of people about their answers. I've learned about successes and failures.

While this book is chock-full of information, ideas, and insights, I don't suggest that it has all the answers. You will learn about other approaches from fellow leaders and from other books. It's important to keep learning.

In structuring *Keeping Good People*, I designed the first section of the book to provide a foundation for the balance of the text. The more we can understand about a problem, any problem, the better we are equipped to respond to it.

Following the discussion of current and future conditions, we will consider a variety of strategic approaches to keeping good people. Our assumption is that you have hired good people to begin with; recruiting and hiring won't be discussed in this book. There is an abundance of material already written about that aspect of human resource management.

People leave employment positions because of internal drives to improve their lot. They also leave because their working conditions are not comfortable for them. There are other reasons, too, like a spouse's transfer to another section of the country, but this book can't possibly deal with all those situations.

Therefore, we're stating up front that this book is not complete. It can't be. The world is changing too rapidly to assert that all the answers on any topic can be locked into one volume. That's why we encourage you to be alert to anything you learn about this topic.

What we will be sharing in the following pages are strategies and techniques that have worked, in one situation or another, for people and organizations just like yours. I hope you have already thought about, and applied, some of what you are about to read. Some of the material in these pages should not be new for you.

As a manager and a leader for most of my career, I have practiced many of the techniques shared in this book. Most of the time they worked. As a full-time consultant to a wide variety of organizations since 1980, I have observed and recommended many more approaches. Most of them worked.

No, not everything you try to do will work just the way you expect it to. It's not a perfect world. Some things are beyond our control, and some situations are a lot more complicated than we may know. Simply put, you just have to gain all the information you can, then apply the strategies that seem to make the most sense at the time.

If you've done your best, be happy with yourself. If your plan worked, great! If it didn't, try something else. Life will have its setbacks. Just because you've perhaps lost one member of your team who was really important to you does not mean your entire organization is falling around you. There are many other good people around you; they need you and your enthusiastic leadership!

My hope is that this book will help you continue to build exciting, vibrant, productive organizations.

One thing this book is not is a recitation of success stories of companies that have kept good people on their teams. I have not cited countless examples for several reasons:

First, just because a company is successful today in a particular endeavor, it does not mean that the company will be as successful in the future. Companies that are successful in one aspect of their activity may not be worthy of note in other aspects.

Second, it is counterproductive to compare yourself to others. Each of us is working with a unique set of circumstances. What makes sense for Company A may be totally wrong for Company B. And, if Company A's executives were asked, they'd probably tell you not to try their way in your situation.

Third, from my experience as a manager and as a consultant, I would encourage every reader of this book to think for himself or herself. Engage in a careful examination of your environment, of your challenges, of your people. Then, with good intentions and knowledge gained from this book and other sources, do what you feel is best for your organization.

You have to take calculated risks to determine what is most appropriate for you and your people. You can't simply "go by the book" when leading a team of people and managing a company. You have to apply your instinct, your "gut feeling" about conditions, to achieve your desired results.

Keeping Good People offers ideas, food for thought. It is up to you to decide which approaches would be most effective for you.

Keeping Good People

SECTION ONE

Chapter 1

Good People
and Their Value
in Organizations

For any kind of an organization to run successfully, several human elements are essential. One is good leadership at the top and, for best results, throughout the organization. A second need is for good management. Third, there must be a team of people with the knowledge, skills, aptitudes, and attitudes to perform at a sufficiently high level of production to accomplish the organization's mission.

The same requirements are there, whether you are running a manufacturing company, a service business, a professional firm, a non-profit organization, an educational institution, a social service agency, a volunteer group, or any other kind of entity. The need is universal.

When we use the term, "good people," we're talking about your employees who have the capability, and use that capability, to perform in a high-achieving manner to accomplish the work of the organization. These are the kinds of people who are sought by managers and human resource professionals. When the recruiting effort is successful, the

3

next objective is to enable the new team member to be as productive as possible...and to keep that person on the team.

What makes these people "good?" There are a number of factors that distinguish what we describe as good people from others. It's a quality issue. The ones who are good are the high performers we would prefer not to lose. They are the people who get the job done.

We find good people in every occupation. There are good people in management, in research and development, in the production area, in sales and marketing, in administrative services, and in the custodial ranks. Each kind of organization has its categories of employee titles and roles, and there are good people in all these places.

Being good does not require any particular level of education or professional credentials. Experience does not automatically make someone a better employee. The difference is how the education and experience are applied.

The speed with which someone works does not necessarily make that person a good employee. Quality is just as important, if not more important, in measuring actual results. Hours worked are not, alone, a performance indicator.

Some people are good because they're so creative, but in another occupation creativity may not be as strong a factor in considering a person's value. Some are good because they can stick with a project and see it through to completion. Others are highly valued because of their ability to solve problems or initiate new projects.

Some people are valuable in organizations because of their ability to communicate, to work well with co-workers, customers, or suppliers. Others are equally valued because of their ability to work independently to get their jobs done.

The assessment of an employee as "good" is a value judgement made by the organization's leadership and others on the team. In making such a determination, there is a recognition that this good employee is one of the more important members of the team, for whatever reason(s). This is one of the people most responsible for the organization accomplishing its goals.

Ideally, all the employees will be good. Working together as a performance team, they get results. We would not want to lose any of them. If we have hired, trained, and managed well, each of our people will be good--highly valued--for one reason or another.

It is these good people we want to keep on our team. They make the difference between us and our competitors. They enable us to do what we are expected to do. If these people are not working on our team, they could be just as successful on some other organization's team.

The Value of Good People

Those we describe as "good people" often set the pace on their work teams. As pacesetters, they inspire and motivate others by their example and by their enthusiasm. Those around them strive more diligently. In some cases, the entire work team is more energetic, more supportive, and more productive.

Research, development, production, and service people are more motivated when working with someone who has demonstrated expertise. Everyone around such a person feels more confident because of the high level of competence shown by one dedicated employee. The quality and accuracy is measurably higher when good technical people are involved.

Sales and marketing efforts are considerably more effective when undertaken by conscientious professionals. Such good people can assure a company an abundance of solid, profitable business that can be sustained over a long period of time.

Creativity and innovation are in high demand in many organizations today. Those who can solve the puzzles, who can aggressively meet the challenges with new and different approaches, can make a significant difference in overall success.

Persistence is valued in many organizations today. The perseverance to stick with a project or task until it is finished is vital. To get things done, methodically following through on routine and special assignments with reliability is important. Practically every team needs good people who can be depended upon.

Accuracy, attention to detail, quality control, careful research and analysis are required in the effective functioning of most organizations. Good people who can perform this kind of work are vital to their continued success.

Each of our good people brings something unique to the work team. They become even more valuable when led by other good people who mold them into highly productive teams. As these good people work cooperatively together, the work gets done, people enjoy what they are doing, and desired results are achieved.

Chapter 2

The Predicament

One of the major challenges facing employers as we shift from the 20th into the 21st century is finding and keeping good employees. While this book will deal primarily with the strategies for *keeping* good employees, it is valuable to gain a solid understanding of the cause of the problem.

Whenever you are trying to solve a problem, be sure you are wrestling with the actual causes, not just the symptoms. Treating symptoms is only a temporary, band-aid solution.

Understanding the challenge of attracting and keeping good people, with its many ramifications, will enable you as an employer and/or organizational leader, to better manage the achievement of desired results. While the problem is not a simple one, some of the potential solutions are not that difficult. A clear vision of the overall situation is helpful to better appreciate the importance of the strategic solutions.

Competition

The predicament we face today is multi-faceted. A major factor is that we are operating in an increasingly competitive environment with seemingly limited resources. Companies are competing vigorously against each other for business...and for resources. Even divisions and departments within companies compete with each other for resources. Interestingly, some corporate units even compete against each other for business or market share in the same industries!

There are other employers out there who would love to have some of your key people working for them. They use all sorts of methods to discover the identity of those good people, then carefully learn how they might persuade those valuable folks to leave you and join them.

The corporate intelligence system is fascinating. It includes in-house recruiters, market and industry analysts, and executive recruiters. Some companies even engage investigative firms to help gather information on competitors and their people. As a former military counterintelligence agent, I can tell you the information is more readily available than you might suspect.

Once your competitors know which of your people they want to "target", the rest of the work is a matter of diligence and patience. Prospective hires are contacted at work, at home, and through various civic, religious, fraternal, or trade/professional relationships. It's open season.

How your people will respond to overtures from prospective employers will depend on how comfortable they are working in your organization. If they feel like productive, satisfied, valued members of your team, they will be less receptive to other offers. If their needs are being met in your environment, if they see opportunities for the future in your system, if they identify closely with you, the invader will have little success in pulling them away from you.

This resistance to outside temptations doesn't just happen. It is the result of the application of a number of deliberate strategies to assure that your good people intentionally remain as vital members of your team.

The invading competitors will look for weaknesses in your armor. They will try to ferret out the problems and concerns your people face, then capitalize on those opportunities to sell your people on the idea of jumping ship.

The weaknesses could be real or imagined. Even the great Greek warrior, Achilles, had his vulnerability. As a defense mechanism, and as a way to better understand your situation, it might be worthwhile to look objectively and critically at your organization. What do you know, or what can you or trusted associates learn, about your weaknesses? Find your holes and plug them before the dike breaks.

The principles and techniques applied to keep good people can be viewed as a defense mechanism. However, everything you do to protect your human resources against encroachment will also strengthen the bonds between you, your people, and your company. This increasing strength will improve your productivity and positively affect your bottom line.

So, if you do the things that legitimately should be done by any prudent businessperson running an organization in these times, your threat from competitors will be minimized.

Career Development Drive

Today's employee wants to achieve the greatest possible results, personally, during his or her career. People will seek the best opportunities they can find to enhance their careers. If people can accomplish their growth objectives with one employer over a long period of time, they will usually remain there to continue growing. If the environment is perceived as restrictive, they will quite naturally seek other opportunities.

It is important to note that people will seek greener pastures even if they merely *perceive* that the environment is restrictive. It doesn't have to be reality, just perception, and the internally-driven employee will move on. The "restrictive" employer will be left with those workers who are less interested in bettering themselves, who are content to remain in the rut of mediocrity.

It's easy to see how companies that are not people-oriented will lose their best talent. It will be hard for them to maintain desired levels of production, quality, and service without superior people to at least lead the effort. Result? The companies that are not people-sensitive eventually fail. There's a moral here.

The best people will seek their best opportunities, just as water seeks its own level. The trend will be toward any kind of movement that the employee believes will strengthen current and/or future career positioning. People will move to positions where they can achieve their personal goals, where they feel most comfortable in being able to make a contribution and have an impact on their work environment.

Indications are we will see a shift away from short-sightedness, looking for the best deal today, to more long-range perspectives. People will more critically examine their opportunities to evaluate realistically what the future may hold. What will they be able to do, how will they be able to grow, how much influence will they have over their work and the work of others?

This kind of shifting for career growth will be seen in all settings, except where the individual feels trapped for some reason. A surprising number of employees feel trapped in their jobs, not able to move. This sense of entrapment causes people to become disinterested and demotivated, with resulting lower productivity and accountability.

It's valuable to understand why some people feel trapped in their jobs. Most often the entrapment is an internal, personal feeling; in other cases, it's very real. Some people are limited by their level of skills or experience. They may not have the formal education they need to compete in a different arena--in their own self-perception and/or in the expectations of society.

The trap could be a result of the Peter Principle. The employee may, in fact, have gone as far as possible. This may, in fact, be true; or the employee may believe other people who suggest in various ways that it might be the case. Self-esteem is so fragile in today's world, that many people don't believe they can pull themselves up by the bootstraps that were used so well just a generation ago.

Others feel trapped because of outside influences, such as a spouse's employment, a desire to keep children in the same school system, or simply being hesitant to make changes in their lives. Regardless of the cause, the resultant behavior is the same. The trapped people will stay where they are reluctantly and resentfully, trigger-ready to move and less dedicated to excelling in their current position.

The feeling of being limited in one's choices builds resentment. We'll see more of these people, who see themselves as being trapped, become increasingly ready to jump ship to a better position as soon as they have an opportunity. They will be driven to make these moves, even though it might not be the best arrangement for them in the long run. There will be a stronger desire for freedom of choice of work and employer.

Shortage of Good People

Part of our challenge stems from the reduction in the quantity of qualified people available to hire. This condition is the result of several factors, some beyond control and some open to remedy (although relatively long- term).

A drop in the birth rate in the late 1950s and early 1960s is causing a significant drop in the numbers of people in the employment pool. This reduction, estimated at 20% below the accustomed rate, has produced a shortfall of five million native-born Americans in the workforce. This impact is being felt strongly in many industries in the 1990s as we experience a shortage in needed entry level workers (18 to 24 age range).

While the birth rate increased after the so-called "baby bust", it did not return to the previous level. We must accept the fact that, for various socio-economic and values reasons, our birth rate will not generate new workers at the same levels as previously enjoyed. Employers will simply have to work with fewer American-born and educated people entering the workforce in the 1990s and early 2000s.

During the upcoming years, the impact of the birth rate decline will be blunted by the proportion of older workers who will remain in the workforce. Many of these senior employees simply want to keep working ("if I retire, I won't have anything to do, so I guess I'll just die"). Others will have to keep working because of inadequate pension planning or support. High achievers who still have things to do before they retire will have a high motivation to remain in their positions. These conditions will generate some interesting, and somewhat predictable, benefits and challenges and difficulties for all sorts of organizations.

You can expect some conflict among your people if older and younger workers have to function together. Different sets of values regarding such things as the work ethic, dress, and other aspects of life may generate friction between these folks. Some of this is inevitable, so you have to be sensitive to the potential problems and deal with them as they arise.

A word of caution: many older employees are taking advantage of early retirement options. They then move into other organizations, often in influential positions, to continue their careers. When considering one of these valuable, experienced people as a new member of your team, ask some questions about their attitudes toward young people and their values in the workplace. Get the concerns out on the table, so you know what you are dealing with.

Note: *you can not, under Federal law, discriminate against an applicant because of age. And not all older workers have* *conflicting attitudes and values with younger workers. Your sensitivity should be not to the person's age, whatever it may be, but to discuss with all applicants their attitudes and beliefs regarding issues involved in the work environment.*

Your job is to build a team of people that can work best together to accomplish your organization's objectives. To do this, you must find the best talent available and get people working together for the common good.

Insufficient Supply of "Good" Workers

Another complication in our formula of "good" workers is the qualifications of people to meet the needs of modern American industry.

One point of debate is what constitutes a good worker. Some point to educational credentials. Others argue that experience makes the difference. Still others seek the hard-to-measure quality of plain old common sense. Few disagree with the value of dedicated, diligent effort applied to get tasks accomplished. Words like loyalty, commitment, caring, quality-consciousness, and an entrepreneurial attitude surface in many conversations.

The quality of the workers available, in practically every field, is seriously below what is needed by today's lean organizations. With the rising cost of just about everything, employers need workers who can handle the tasks that were previously done by more people with less skills. We are becoming much more of a technology-based work society; the people we hire must be able to use Computer-Numerically-Controlled (CNC) production machinery, robots, and a host of other automation devices found in almost every aspect of our operations.

The bottom line, frankly, is the combination of the worker's knowledge, acquired skills, and personal attitudes. With the right combination of these qualities, people can do amazing things. Following effective leaders, workers with these qualities can surpass the productivity levels currently seen in most workplaces.

So, where's our problem? Is it a lack of knowledge? Do our workers not have the necessary skills to get the job done? Are we suffering from attitude problems in American organizations? Do our leaders fall short in responding to their opportunity?

The answer, unfortunately, is "yes" to all the questions.

The Knowledge Deficiency

Unfortunately, too many workers (including many who are recent high school graduates) can not read, write, or reason well enough to fill the kinds of jobs that are available. This condition makes those who can perform even more valuable to current and prospective employers. It also presents challenges for employers who want to be good corporate citizens and hire the people who need jobs. A lot of training and retraining has to be done.

Across the country, community leaders are beginning to realize that their public (and in many cases, private and parochial) school systems are simply not getting their job done. It's become serious enough for the clarion call to sound forth from Washington. The federal government can't get the job done alone, however: it's a distinctly local problem with local solutions.

As our students compete against their counterparts from other industrialized nations, we are embarrassed more often than not by a poor showing. Too few school systems place sufficient emphasis on academics. Many are so distracted by sports, local school system politics, or the local momentum that they automatically promote/graduate students who simply can not perform to basic literacy levels.

It's been pointed out that our literacy problem begins in the home. Today's parents don't read enough to their children, let alone set an example by reading themselves. Aside from a few basic educational programs for pre-schoolers, television programming presents a serious barrier to literacy.

The results are that Johnny can't read, write, compute, or think upon graduation from high school. Some college graduates aren't of much higher caliber. If this sounds like an indictment of our educational system, so be it! When the graduates have trouble completing employment application forms, there's something wrong.

The Partnership Solution

Employers are beginning, finally, to complain--some loudly--that the graduating seniors aren't prepared to enter the workforce. It's gone beyond head shaking and tsk-tsking. Too many of today's graduates aren't able to perform the basic work asked of them by employers. This makes this next generation of American workers/potential leaders unemployable.

With the quantitative shortage of raw material, an increasing number of employers are having to invest stockholders' dollars in providing basic training in literacy and mathematics--just to educate employees to the level where they can perform productive work!

When high school graduates can not write a simple report, letter, or even an autobiographical essay, we have a problem that must be addressed. When these new adults can not balance a checkbook, something's wrong. When they can't read the directions to learn how to operate a machine, their productive capacity is limited. When they don't have enough knowledge to serve as a foundation for learning new skills, it's clear that we have a serious problem.

This problem is complicated by our rapidly-changing technology. It's enough of a challenge for businesses to keep up; our schools are pitifully far behind in most cases. I remember taking a computer course in graduate school, learning technology that was already out-of-date. From what I've seen, the situation hasn't changed much.

The solution, it seems, is for business leaders to work more closely with those responsible for the education of young people about to enter the workforce--at high school and college levels. And educators must be not only receptive, but eager for this invaluable input. This vital partnership must focus on innovative ways to effectively prepare America's new worker to respond positively to the challenges of the work environment.

Part of the problem with this almost idealistic strategy is that too many employers are overwhelmed by the training and development needs within their own organizations. They are not equipped, with insight or talent, to help the schools help them. It's the classic dilemma of the chicken and the egg. Yet, it is a cycle that must be broken!

All of us must take our share of the responsibility to increase the amount and quality of usable knowledge being absorbed by today's students. Yes, it's time to get back to the basics (again), providing both theoretical and practical knowledge that will be of value in the working--and personal growth worlds.

Since it will take time to break through the barriers of habitual mediocrity in so many of our schools, employers must devote resources to helping new (and older) employees learn more of the basic knowledge that will enable them to excel on the job. The remedial and growth work in this field is being undertaken in corporate environments and in the classrooms of community colleges nationally.

Our efforts must not stop. There is too much at stake. When working with your employees who lack some of the knowledge they need, don't just give up on them. Don't just let them languish at a low level position forever. From the executive, staff, and supervisory levels, work together to help each of your people become stronger tomorrow than today.

The Immigration Factor

Complicating the scenario described above is the increasing influx of immigrant labor. These new Americans sometimes come with fine skills and experience, sometimes not. The great majority of them come without knowledge of the English language, let alone formal education within the structure that we take for granted in the United States.

These immigrants may have trouble communicating, but many of them have a lot to offer today's America. Often they come with a set of valuable or adaptable skills. They are, in most cases, accustomed to working hard. It just comes naturally to them, arising from a sense of necessity for survival. The basic values are strong...and compatible with those sought by employers.

The problem is that many of them lack the knowledge to be able to communicate effectively on-the-job. Troubles around the world will increase immigration to the United States, and this will increase the proportion of our workforce with a desperate need for basics in their educational background.

Employers, hopefully in cooperation with local educational institutions, will have to enable these people to increase their knowledge so they may interact and become productive in our English-speaking economy. These people must quickly learn English as a second language...while learning what is expected of them in an employment environment.

With the incapacity of some schools to respond adequately to the need, or in areas where appropriate schools simply don't exist, employers have their work cut out for them. Part of the challenge here will be to educate these people in communication, community behaviors, and the accomplishment of productive tasks.

A key area to watch is that people with strong work ethics are not negatively influenced by native Americans more oriented to a get-by attitude. Some immigrant workers display a stronger sense of the "American Work Ethic" than their American counterparts.

Employers hiring non-native Americans to strengthen their labor force should be sensitive to the cultural differences between so-called "mainstream Americans" and those peoples from other countries. In some cases the values are quite similar; in others, they are markedly different--which could have a dramatic effect on labor relations and productivity.

The Skills Gap

People need certain skills to get their jobs done. During earlier periods in our country's history, the emphasis was on the skills of the craftsman. Young people learned from their parents, or other journeymen, crafts such as blacksmithing, mold making, clock repair, tool and die making, and the creation of fine clothing. Offspring often followed in the footsteps of their parents, or at least a relative or neighbor.

Today, it's much different. We learn skills in trade or vocational schools or in apprenticeship programs, usually created and managed by industry trade associations as a feeder system to support member companies. Skill-building also takes place within the industrial setting, but it is a time-consuming and costly endeavor. In our environment of cost-consciousness, many employers prefer to "steal" competent skilled people from other companies rather than invest in their in-house development.

Those companies that do take the time and other valuable resources to build skills among their people reap the benefits from their proficiency. At the same time, they are forced into paying higher levels of compensation and giving other benefits to keep those skilled people from being attracted away by competitors.

Even with all our advances in technology, there is still a need for skilled craftsmen. In the tire industry, for example, the molds for the tire treads are carefully carved by people who have learned their skills over many years. It is estimated that there are fewer than forty of these people in the country, and no school training programs to prepare young people to take their places over time.

Tool and die makers fit into a similar category. New technology helps them learn and perform their work, but the initial learning process is a long one. Relatively few high school students set their sights on becoming tool and die makers. The machine tool industries don't hold the attraction for young people that they did a generation or two ago. Companies in this field, and other trades, have to do more aggressive recruiting today.

Today many of our young people are aimed toward the computer-oriented fields. This is not inappropriate, since there is so much done with the aid of computers. In fact, by necessity, faced with a shortage of skilled people and an economic pressure to produce with lower labor costs, many industries have found ways to produce goods using technology instead of people.

While robotics increases manufacturing efficiency, it has not really decreased the number of jobs. People are still needed to set-up and service the robots.

On the surface technological advances may appear beneficial. However, now employers are having difficulty finding people who are educationally and technically qualified to operate the new equipment. An increasing amount of work is performed by computer numerically controlled machines (CNC), for example, but employers have difficulty finding people who can understand the work to be done...and operate these often complex machines.

Attitudes

The attitudes of our workers, especially our good people, and their leaders, have a considerable impact on our potential for high achievement. Simultaneously, attitudes have a significant influence on whether our good people stay with us or go somewhere else.

People are sensitive to the attitudes of those around them. Good people, who are seeking higher levels of accomplishment than their fellow employees, are sensitive to the attitudes of their co-workers. They are most influenced, however, by the attitudes and the actions of other high achievers and of their leaders.

Strong, effective, focused leadership is vital in organizations today, be they for-profit, non-profit, governmental, or other types. Leadership is different than management. Being a leader implies being more involved with your people and what they are doing. As a leader, you set the pace to make things happen.

Managers are responsible for the most appropriate allocation of available resources to assure that assigned tasks are accomplished, with the expected quantity, quality, and timeliness. Among the resources managed is the human resource: your people.

Both roles are interchangeable, even though they are different. While some people have a greater propensity to take charge and make things happen, leadership and management are learned skills.

When you're in charge, people look to you for answers, direction, guidance, expertise, and maturity, and stability. If they don't get what they are seeking in your organization, you can legitimately expect them to look elsewhere for it.

If you can demonstrate the attitudes that good people look for in their leaders, you will attract and keep the kinds of employees who can move your organization to continued high achievement.

Beyond attitude is performance. You have to do those things that good people expect from their organization. While you probably won't be able do meet *every* expectation your people have, the essence will be in the way you meet those expectations you *can* recognize and fulfill.

Chapter 3

The Competitive Environment

Competition is an accepted behavior in America. It's part of our national culture. We learn competitiveness as children and it becomes a natural part of our existence.

Each of us competes against others in many aspects of our lives: in sports, in school work, in striving for a better place in line at the check-out counter, and vying for a more advantageous position in traffic as we race toward work--or home--each day. We compete with ourselves to do things better, faster, or cheaper than we did them previously.

So, it's quite normal for people to compete in the work environment. People compete for the best parking spaces or office spaces. They compete for attention from the boss or favored customer. Promotions and special assignments are considered competitive arenas. The winners "earn" the benefits that come with winning. Losers, if the losing is perceived as bitter, may leave the playing field to seek another opportunity to compete with a chance of winning.

We compete, in the business world, for a wide range of resources to accomplish our objectives. Among these resources are capital, materials, space, time, and people. That's about all we really have to work with. Our results come as a result of how we apply those resources.

Our competitive strengths come from efficient and effective use of resources by people. The way we utilize our human resource is really the last frontier of competition. People contribute strengths such as creativity, the development and application of technology, and task accomplishment focused on the achievement of results.

Essentially, then, to compete today we must earn the greatest possible return on our investment in human resources. The application of other resources is dependent on our having strong people on our team.

The Competition for Good People

It is an accepted fact in organizational growth, development, achievement, and stability, that we need to attract the best possible people to work productively as a smooth-functioning team.

Companies invest thousands of dollars in recruiting efforts to attract the quality of applicants they seek. This is expected in the personnel marketplace. Employers must aggressively seek the people they want and need. No longer can we expect superior applicants to be knocking at our door. We have to go out and find them.

Good people can be found on college campuses, in high schools and vocational schools, working for other employers, and within our own organization. And here's where the competition starts. Other employers also know where those fine people are, and they want to hire them, too. There are only so many people available. In the decade of the 1990s, and probably beyond, it's a seller's market.

Many companies compete for the eager, receptive college graduates ready to leap off the campus into job opportunities that are beyond their parents' wildest dreams. These often well-equipped and malleable young people are potentially strong assets for the companies that hire them. They have a great deal to offer.

College seniors are looking very carefully at the options available with employers hungry for their talent and energy. They respond to high salary offers that make them look successful in the eyes of their peers (there's that competitive nature again). But, they are also concerned about the quality of the company, the personal growth opportunity, and the long-range potential.

While they realize they may have a number of jobs during their career, many graduates seek situations that will not require them to jump from company to company...at least not for a while. We'll see a shift toward stability as America's young people search for security in their lives.

Good people working for other companies are often receptive to overtures from interested employers. We have a natural tendency to better ourselves, particularly if we can do it with the security of stability and strength.

Yes, there are many good people who are accurately described as risk takers. These particularly aggressive folks will probably go into business for themselves, so think carefully before trying to recruit the independence-oriented entrepreneurial mavericks. You may lose them before you're ready to let them go.

Recruiting people already employed by other companies will be increasingly difficult as employers struggle to hold on to them. Recruiters will be challenged to show significant advantages to entice people to make career changes. Employers will become alert to the constant competitive environment in which we will all operate in the 1990s and early 2000s.

In their efforts to find the best people, employers would be well-advised to look inside their own organizations. Some of your employees may be targets of outside recruitment efforts, while you overlook their potential. Before looking outside, consider the value of your own team members. You may have some wonderful talent, anxious to stay with you to make even more of a difference for their employer.

A word of warning: don't take for granted that your best people will stay with you. Continue to reinforce their value, their opportunity, their mutually-beneficial long-term relationship with you. When you begin taking them for granted, you open the door for the competition to come a-courting.

How to Attract Good People

Part of keeping good people is attracting the right ones in the first place. The things you do to make your company more appealing for outsiders will also enhance the value of employment for those already on your team. So, there are multiple reasons for making yourself look good as an employer of choice people. Create the right kind of image, and your recruitment efforts will be more successful.

There are numerous methods for spreading the positive word about employment at your company. Recruiters usually think first about displays and interviews on college campuses, at trade shows, and at vocational schools. Those are fine, for targeted efforts, but your company has to have a positive image to support those sales pitches.

The values shared by the majority of the good people you want to attract and keep lean heavily toward employers being solid corporate citizens. It will become increasingly important for companies to demonstrate their civic responsibility by involvement in community activities, respected contributions to industry and trade associations, and caring for their employees.

Some of these efforts will offer opportunities to get your people involved. This makes them a part of the good things their employer is doing, strengthening the bonds of long-term relationships. Some examples are support of walkathons for charitable causes, United Fund drives and organizations, and urban redevelopment programs. There are many other worthwhile endeavors deserving of corporate--and employee--participation.

Your corporate image is enhanced by good publicity, advertising, and public relations. Whether you engage an outside publicist or manage your promotion program internally, strive to gain positive exposure in the media. Share with news representatives information about new products or services, achievements by your people, plans for expansion, and anything else that might earn you some news or feature coverage.

Don't concentrate only on the dramatic stories that make a big splash. A lot of little items will be as effective... or even more effective. Think of the power of spaced repetition the psychologists tell us about. Repeated positive exposure of your company name, even for such things as sponsorship of Little League or the high school play, will remind people of your positioning as a good employer.

Other opportunities for valuable exposure (which may also generate positive publicity) include talks to local civic groups, and seminars at conventions and conferences, testimony before legislative committees. Consider also sponsorship or support of educational programs such as Junior Achievement at the high school level and academic groups at colleges and universities.

Don't overlook the needs of elementary and middle schools in your community; your help will be sincerely appreciated and may influence a parent or older sibling to consider joining you. Beyond mere financial support, share your expertise, your company's talent, insight (participate in career days), and equipment. [That obsolete piece of equipment might be really appreciated by a vocational school or college in your community.] Earn a reputation as an employer supporting quality education.

Offer your company's expertise as a resource to news media such as metropolitan daily newspapers, business newspapers and magazines, trade journals, radio talk shows, and television news shows. Being recognized as a quotable authority never hurts, especially when one of your valued people represents you as an industry expert. Tapping your people for such service serves to recognize them personally, too.

When your people are involved in the ways described above, don't hesitate to share their contribution with others. Internally, you can express your pride through your company newsletter or bulletin board displays.

Consider ways you can brag, tastefully, about your people to your customers and prospective customers. For example, if someone is quoted in an industry magazine, you could reprint the article (with permission), highlight your company representative's comments, and send the marked article to interested customers.

Seek appropriate publicity for promotions, new appointments, discoveries, inventions, and significant accomplishments. If one of your people is elected or appointed to an office in a trade or professional association, recognize that achievement and dedication inside your company and to the public. Look for creative ways to spread the good word about what your people and your company are doing.

The same positive exposure you get in the "outside world" will strengthen your bonds internally with your people. Take advantage of every chance you can find to reinforce how important each one of your team members is to your organization.

You can build employee loyalty by merely writing a letter to your involved team member expressing your appreciation, support, and admiration. You can make an even stronger impression by sending the letter to the employee's home. Be sure to put a copy in the personnel file. These efforts will be well received by the concerned employee, and will also be noticed by others. People watch how others are treated; your actions should always generate good feelings.

Be Worthy of Good People

To attract and keep good people, you must have something to offer them. They must see joining you as being a positive career move. This means your company must be perceived as a fine place to work, from the perspectives of being a comfortable environment, providing quality products and services, and being good for the reputation of the people who work there.

More and more, people are asking the all-important question of "what's in it for me." If they don't see the positive aspects of working for you, on a short-term and on a long-term basis, don't expect to keep them.

In the coming decades, we will not see the same level of employee loyalty to a particular employer that we have seen in the past. Any employer desiring that kind of dedication will have to earn it. Every day.

Show that you are a solid company with a clear sense of the future. If you don't already have one, write a mission statement or statement of purpose. Hint: if you involve a number of your people in this effort, the statement will have much more meaning and impact. People support what they help to create. And, by sharing the visionary effort with others, you gain their perspectives as input and express your feeling of the value of their contribution.

If you are not a solid company, perhaps a start-up entrepreneurship or an older company in need of a shot of revitalization, make this clear to the good people you have and the ones you're trying to recruit. Your circumstances may call for some special kinds of folks; the cream will rise to the top and the talent you need will respond to the need.

Whatever your particular situation, be deliberate about what you are trying to do. People want to know there's someone at the helm, guiding their ship through the storm or through the racing channels. Knowing you are there, doing your job with a strong sense of purpose and focus, will help build confidence in you and in the organization. That level of confidence is vital if you want to attract and keep good people.

Take pride in your corporate achievements. Enable your people to do the same. Share with them every positive aspect you can think of. Empower them to stand tall--in your industry, in the community, in their families. As humans, we like to have pride in our affiliations, in our work, and in ourselves. We like to know that we're meeting the challenges of life and striving to make a positive difference.

Anything you can do to reinforce feelings of pride, satisfaction, and achievement will strengthen your position in reaching and keeping the people who can lead your company into the next century.

Separate Yourself from the Crowd

What is unique about your company? Why should someone work for you instead of working for your competitor or a company in another industry? How can you establish your organization, and your opportunity, as being different from other alternatives in the employment marketplace?

Your better applicants are going to compare the offers they receive. They will look for "comfort factors" as they make their choices. They will also look for "discomfort factors" that may inspire a negative decision.

In the area of comfort factors, it is valuable to consider all the things we've been discussing in this chapter. Aggressively promote the positive aspects of your company, both internally and externally. Your external efforts will help attract the people you want, as well as support the image that will encourage people to stay with you because of the public perception of your company. Your internal efforts will generate positive feelings, reinforcing your current employees' decision to continue as part of your team.

When applicants visit your offices, they are judging your company by what they see. When you go to work tomorrow, look objectively at your neighborhood, grounds, building(s), reception area or lobby, and the offices an applicant is likely to visit. You may be surprised at what you see. Look critically; your applicants will.

One suggestion might be to have management and leadership books on display in your office. Of special importance will be those dealing with human resource issues. The books in your office send messages to visitors about your interests. Show them what is important to you. You might want to put this book and a copy of *The Process of Excelling* in plain sight.

Show visitors you keep current in your field. Current periodicals, which may be familiar to them, should be displayed in your office and/or in the waiting room. The good people you want to attract will be concerned that the company's leadership is on the cutting edge.

These ideas will help you show your concerns and interests to your current employees as well. Of course, if you read these publications and discuss the books or articles with your people, you will verify that you really care about what you are doing. You will also serve as an example for your people; there is a much greater chance people will read and learn if they know the boss does, and that the boss asks questions and raises issues from those publications.

Another comfort factor is your company's reputation for quality in its products and services. It has to be real, not just a sham or cover-up so things look good on the surface. To earn and maintain this reputation, it's imperative that you and other leaders in your company devote a lot of serious attention to quality. If you are sincere, and if you really focus on quality, you will earn respect and admiration for the way things are done in your organization.

That admiration and respect will motivate your good people, who are striving to deserve that reputation, to stay with you. Success begets success. If they're achieving, they will want to stay and achieve more as long as they are challenged and feel positive about the experience.

Focus on People Factors

Attitude is perhaps the single greatest determinant of decisions in our lives. We do things because we like something associated with those things. We avoid things about which we have a negative attitude. When we examine attitudes in the workplace, we soon focus on morale and team spirit.

Not everyone is going to be excited about work. Not everyone is going to throw total energy into being a team player. Each person comes from a different direction. Your challenge, perhaps obligation, is to pull them together so your people are all going the same direction.

So many books and magazine articles point to what has happened in Japan as being a good example for us to follow. Personally, I am a bit uncomfortable about that. Many of the management techniques that have made Japanese industry strong originated in the United States. While the Japanese have applied those techniques diligently, Americans went off in search of new fads, new approaches. What works is basic, down-to-earth caring involvement with the people who make progress and achievement possible.

For illustration, I will yield my resistance to "Japanese answers." Consider these guiding principles from Matsushita Electric (Panasonic), where morale remains very high:

- respect
- awards
- communication
- courtesy
- discussion
- negotiation
- consensus
- loyalty to employees
- socializing

- training
- few direct orders
- long-term thinking
- hope for the future
- innovative freedom
- job permanence
- stable conditions
- clearly assigned responsibilities
- special welcome to new people
- lots of smiles
- plenty of please and thank-you
- thoughtfulness and consideration
- receptiveness to criticism
- generous help with retirement
- dedication
- determination
- discipline
- industrious hard work

It isn't necessary to have pep rallies to get people turned-on. People will do that for themselves...if they perceive a positive environment for the company and for themselves. People will get excited, and maintain a high level of enthusiasm, if they see results and feel the caring from senior management.

Your People Are Competing

As working people, we compete. Using all the resources at our disposal, we go after the best jobs, the highest income, the greatest status, and the strongest opportunity to make a valuable contribution to our employer and society. We strive to control our own destiny.

Look at your good people, those folks you want to keep on your team. How sensitive, how aware are you of their striving? Wise leaders will use all their communications skills to observe how people are competing, what is important to them. Ask questions. Listen. Listen some more.

If you want to keep your good people, give them as much of what they want as you can. Understand how they are, consciously or unconsciously, competing with each other for attention, favor, opportunity. Guide their competition to be positive for them and for your organization.

Encouraging people to put forth their best effort can easily produce winners. But, in competitive environments, you may also produce losers. If two people are competing for the same job, you may well want to keep them both. Consider what you can do for the person(s) who don't get the choice assignment or the promotion. If you aren't able to do something to make your selection a win-win situation, you risk losing those who don't "win" the one position open.

Give people alternatives of relatively similar significance. If someone doesn't get an expected or desired promotion, what else can you offer? A challenging special assignment? Promise of the next open promotion? Be careful not to make promises you can't keep. Don't manipulate the system beyond reasonable limits for personal reasons. Stay focused on the long-term. Know that different people want, or will be satisfied with, different kinds of rewards. Learn enough about each of your people that you can respond to individual needs.

Some people want higher positions just to have a more important position in the organizational hierarchy. They like to see their name in a box that's further up on the chart. Climbing that kind of a career ladder is paramount to some people. For others, the position they hold isn't that important. Don't make assumptions. What's good for Gail Goose isn't necessarily what Gil Gander wants.

There are those who are driven to earn as much money as possible. Very little else even matters. They will be happy with a lesser position, very little recognition, low status, and so forth...if they have a strong income. There are a number of different ways to structure compensation packages to attract and hold good people. See chapter nine for a deeper treatment of this issue.

Status and prestige are highly important for some of your good people. They don't need a higher position, necessarily, or obscene amounts of money. Perhaps they want the perceived high and influential status of a legislative lobbyist. Rubbing elbows with all those powerful politicians is reward enough. Others like titles like "assistant to the president", regardless of the power or the income. Some folks are motivated merely by having a beautiful, embossed, multi-color business card. Feeling important, and/or being perceived by others as being important, is paramount.

With others, their status is more internal. They feel more significant when they get things done. They thrive on the job, the task and the results achieved. These folks compete more with themselves and the challenge or importance of the task. Their focus is often on improving their own performance rather than "beating" someone else.

Included in our country's diverse workforce are people who have an extraordinary level of social consciousness. They compete for opportunities to make significant contributions to society through their work. They are usually attracted, and bound to, organizations that are engaged in work for the public good. The range is wide today, including environmental protection agencies and companies, social service groups, health care, and the like. They are found in non-service settings as well, but prefer to work for companies that demonstrate their social conscience.

Many creative people compete for positions where they can design or produce something that will be a long-term benefit for society. Included in this category are people like architects, artists, teachers, landscapers, and many other career paths that provide goods or services for the common good and enjoyment of others.

Today's enlightened worker wants to control his or her own destiny. It's not enough to work for a company forever just because your parent or some other relative spent a lifetime there. Few people want to jump from job to job. Most people want to be independent and strong enough to make their own decisions regarding their employment, career path, and future.

We Compete to Keep People

Efforts to attract, inspire, and keep the best people we can find must be continuous. It's almost like creating a force field of protection around our people. They are "captive" as long as we continue our activity to maintain that force field. As soon as we relax our diligence, the competition can move right in to take advantage of all we have done to cultivate a fine employee.

You will find competition coming from four different sources. The first source I describe as being non-specific. The second source is companies within your industry. Third is employers from other industries. The fourth is from within our own organization.

Our non-specific competition is an internal attitude that can easily lead to pro-active or reactive behavior. If our key employee is not satisfied, there will be a greater receptivity to alternative employment. Under these attitudinal circumstances, people are apt to be less productive--less motivated to work for the common good of the organization, much less themselves.

When there are no specific outside attractions, the competitor is really without form. The alienation feelings will often lead the employee to seek other opportunities, almost indiscriminately. The grass begins to look greener on the other side of the fence. You risk losing the employee because of what has happened, or hasn't happened, within your own environment. As the expression goes, you can be your own worst enemy. You're actually pushing these people out, rather than having them attracted out by competitors.

The competition for good people you face in your own industry is dangerous. The companies that compete against you for sales and market share also want your people. You have trained them; they've proven their worth to an employer in your field. Even more valuable, perhaps, is their knowledge of your systems, customers, pricing, and a myriad of other facts that comprise corporate intelligence.

The risk here is that you could lose far more than a valued employee. And, what is worse, the employee could be "used" by the competitor, then discarded. With the pressure of competition today, some companies are offering hard-to-turn-down incentives to capture employees of other companies in their field. They parasitically suck all the worthwhile knowledge they can from the unsuspecting employee, then terminate the employment. The poor drained employee is out on the street, while the parasite takes advantage of all the new knowledge and insight gained.

Many employers today feel it is heartily advised to build strong feelings of loyalty and competitiveness among their workforce. The fierce attachment to their company is directed against the competitors. This us-against-them power is aimed at encouraging innovation, efficiency, cunning, effectiveness, and profitability to make the host employer successful against the "hated" competitors. That same energy also stimulates resistance against even the hint of going over to the other side. Not wanting to be traitors, employees who leave the company also leave the industry.

Many companies deliberately recruit outside their industry. They seek applicants with applicable skills, talent, knowledge, background, or training. Bringing fresh perspectives from a different industry might enable a new employee to help keep the organization alert, innovative, responsive, and generally on the cutting edge. Hiring people with extensive experience in the same industry could spawn in-breeding and tunnel vision.

Some companies have grown so large that they have a number of separate divisions or subsidiaries. The people who operate the various entities may not know each other, particularly below the senior management levels. Even though they have the same core ownership, they function much like different companies in separate industries.

These divisions may try to recruit people away from each other. They can offer the attractiveness of being able to continue with the same health plan, the same retirement program, and other similar comfort factors. Sometimes they can even remain in the same city.

This inter-divisional recruiting can be healthy for cross-training and cross-divisional cooperation. But, it can also cause serious conflicts. Any such recruiting and transferring of people on a temporary or permanent basis, should be done above board with full knowledge and communication by the appropriate officials in each entity.

Appreciate the fact that we are operating in a multi-faceted, multi-dimensional environment. While you should not spend your time looking over your shoulder for your competitors, know that they are there. Make your strategic decisions and implement them as if the competition is right behind you. If you don't, they'll be passing you before you know it.

Chapter 4

What Good People Want

Understanding and appreciating what good people want from their managers and employing organizations is an important first step to meeting those expectations.

In the preceding chapters, we have touched on a number of the desires of good people. Some of these may have been new discoveries for you; most should be "old news." That employees want status, rewards, opportunities, recognition, and similar returns for their investment of time and energy should not be a surprise.

Astute managers know already what needs to be done. They know how to treat their people. Leaders of organizations know what their people want; they just don't concentrate seriously on meeting those needs. Let's gain a better perspective of human needs and how they are met in the workplace.

Understanding Human Needs

Many have struggled to explain the range of human needs, but Abraham H. Maslow's hierarchy of needs is the most representative and the most helpful in our gaining an understanding of what good people want.

Maslow placed all needs into rankings shown as levels. He explained that people will strive first to satisfy basic needs, then once those needs are satisfied will focus on meeting higher level needs. The degree to which each need level must be satisfied before it no longer motivates behavior depends upon the psychological and emotional make-up of each individual.

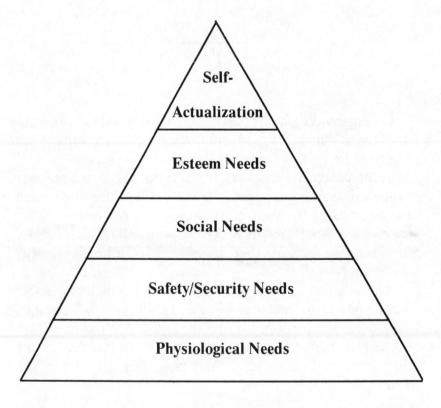

Maslow's Hierarchy of Needs

Initially, psychological needs such as adequate food, air, water, shelter, rest, and clothing (the things needed for physical survival) motivate behavior. In other words, if a person does not have sufficient food, water, clothing or shelter to live in, their behavior is directed at the acquisition of such survival needs. A person does not search for much else until these needs are met.

When sufficient physiological survival means are acquired, they no longer motivate behavior. Then safety and security needs become the motivators. Safety needs include knowing one's physical, emotional, and financial survival are not in jeopardy immediately or in the near future. At this stage, the person seeks avoidance of sources of anxiety or fear, along with the security needs of an organized, stable, predictable environment. Job security fulfills a safety/security need.

These two Maslow levels constitute a group of needs which predispose the individual to be self oriented. In other words, the person experiences life in general and all situations from a *self* oriented perspective.

Continually looking out for self survival, physical as well as emotional, is extremely stressful. Therefore, an organizational environment which either by design or accident induces fear of emotional safety is an environment which drains energy from employees. This energy could otherwise be applied to job productivity.

Such stressful environments do exist in American business today. Consider the feelings of employees of organizations in the midst of merger. How about dictatorial, authoritarian environments designed to keep control through intimidation? Such environments push employees directly into their most unproductive fear state, reducing their productivity, their satisfaction, and their desire to remain in that job.

Beyond Self to Others

Once the person's basic needs, as described by Maslow's first two levels, are satisfied, the employee's perspective broadens to include relationships with other people.

Now the concern is the fulfillment of social needs such as belongingness and love. Close relationships with friends, spouse and family, and fellow employees become important. These needs are met by giving and receiving love, both in the larger sense of friendship and the more intense sense of affection.

At this stage, people have a strong need to be accepted by others, to belong to a group. There is a desire for active participation: the individual contributes something valuable to the work group, and the group recognizes the contribution as worthwhile. Getting employees involved and building a sense of teamness helps fulfill this vital human need.

Employees at this level of needs motivation and perspective require an entirely different organizational reward system, different work structure, different manager and supervisory and peer interactions. Since the respect and approval of others is important, the employee becomes positively motivated by the approval of management and the organization as a whole.

So, we see that employees want to fulfill basic safety and survival needs through physical comforts, security, and financial reward. Once these needs are met, which happens fairly quickly in most employments, the employee's concern is with the fulfillment of social and emotional needs.

Esteem Needs

Once the employee has satisfied social needs, esteem needs become important. Having a high self-regard and having respect for others are representative of this level.

At this stage, the employee is most concerned with self-concept. Self-estimations of strength, confidence, freedom, importance are supplemented by others' recognition of one's status, prestige, reputation, importance, competence, and value.

Respect from others becomes increasingly important. Employees are motivated by feelings of personal competence and self confidence, which can be validated and enhanced by their supervisors. When you express your respect for someone's ability, demonstrate your confidence in the employee, and show your appreciation and support, you help fulfill the esteem need.

When a person's self esteem needs are met, it is an easy and comfortable progression for that person to be able to build the esteem of others. Without that strong inner sense of personal worth, it is much more difficult--if not impossible-- for one to be concerned with the esteem of others. This is why it is important for managers and supervisors, those in leadership positions, to have high self esteem. (See *Appendix C* for an in-depth discussion of self esteem in the corporate setting.)

Self-Actualizing Employees

We now have behavior motivated by self esteem and self actualization needs, a perspective which re-introduces a strong self influence. Behavior is motivated by a sense of making a significant contribution and attaining a high level of self worth.

Self actualization needs motivate individuals toward behavior which stretches them to achieve all they are capable of achieving. Creative expression and greater realization of personal potential become paramount.

It's important for us to recognize that employees at this level of motivation are again more self-oriented. However, a major difference is that the direction for the behavior comes from making a contribution, helping to achieve worthwhile objectives that validate a purpose for one's life.

Employees at this mature level of motivation require more opportunities for involvement and increasing organizational flexibility. The organizational structure, management style, work structure and methods, must change responsively to create and maintain a motivational environment. People must feel encouraged to find ways to realize their work potential, comfortably within the "system." Sometimes the system must change.

An organization that is very authoritarian, that sends the do-as-you're-told message, is non-motivational for these employees. As a matter of fact, these employees may appear as non-conformists or renegades. Because these employees are motivated by self esteem, they tend to think for themselves and see beyond the organization's parameters.

So why would your organization want such employees? Because they are internally motivated. They are the self-starters the self-learners, the independent thinkers who are motivated to make a contribution to society and to your organization. Give them flexibility to be creative. Give them space to think. Encourage their contributions, their thoughts, and their vision. You will not need to concern yourself with motivation.

Any or all of these needs, from the basic physiological needs to the highest level self-actualization needs, may be satisfied through interaction with others in the workplace. These needs are not mutually exclusive; the mix is different for different people. While we said above that once a need is satisfied it can no longer motivate behavior, this does not mean that the person will never have to satisfy that need again.

So the message to organizations desiring to keep people and to keep them productive is to encourage employee development through these various motivational levels. The strategies outlined in this book are designed to help you do just that.

Specific Action Steps

The Maslow hierarchy and other theories have considerable value in helping us understand human wants and needs. The application of this knowledge is most critical for those charged with leading organizations and keeping good people.

Direct supervisors of good people are the vital link between the organization's philosophy and the way things are actually done. Supervisors must understand and appreciate what their people want from them before they can meet those needs. To look at practical applications of needs motivation theories, quite a bit of research has been done.

In the late 1940s, a study was conducted to learn what motivates people in work organizations. Researchers were interested in how workers would respond, but also whether their supervisor's perceptions of the wants were consistent.

People in a wide variety of work settings were surveyed, as were their direct supervisors. Their responses were compared with some surprising results. This research study has been repeated a number of times over the years with the same results.

Respondents were given a list of motivational factors and asked to rank them in their order of importance. The workers were asked to prioritize them from their perspective. The supervisors were asked to rank them in the order they believed the workers would prioritize them.

As you can see from the chart below, the results were dramatically different. Clearly, the supervisors responding to the survey do not have a realistic understanding of what really motivates their people!

Motivational Factor	Workers' Response	Supervisors' Response
good working conditions	9	4
feeling "in" on things	2	10
tactful disciplining	10	7
full appreciation for work done	1	8
management loyalty to workers	8	6
good wages	5	1
promotion and growth	7	3
help on personal problems	3	9
job security	4	2
interesting work	6	5

Note that the factors the workers ranked 1-2-3 were the same ones that the supervisors ranked 8-9-10!

Let's consider the strongest motivators:

1. Employees want to receive feedback on how they are doing. This means that supervisors--in fact, all managers--need to provide recognition of achievement or even just progress toward agreed-upon goals. Without feedback and recognition, workers will have only a marginal commitment to the job. Alienation from supervisors and the organization increases. When commitment and recognition level is low, workers will seek recognition elsewhere--perhaps from outside the organization. This could mean heavier labor-management polarization or workers leaving for other employment.

To overcome such situations, or perceptions, management may need to modify communications systems to provide stronger feedback in a continual and consistent manner. Supervisors can provide motivation by evaluating results of work directly with employees.

2. People want to feel involved in the job to the point of designing the job and establishing goals and objectives. Your employees are human beings, not just numbers or cogs in a machine. They have ideas about how things should be done and questions about why certain things are done or are not done.

Employees are closest to the work for which they are responsible. They want to perform that work in the best way possible. They have the potential (Maslow's self-actualization level) and desire to use it. They *want* to be involved. Thus, supervisors can motivate workers by asking them to set their work goals and to suggest better ways to do things.

3. People want help on personal problems. This doesn't mean that the supervisor must become a social worker. It does suggest that employees want the boss to care about them as individuals. Today's manager must invest a significant amount of time in advising, counseling, coaching, guiding, training, and listening. Be sensitive and understanding. Help people over the rough spots and help them do their best.

Employees who are helped to perform well feel better about themselves, feel more secure, and receive positive feedback from others. It's easy to see how these feelings fit right into the Maslow hierarchy. The key is for supervisors to appreciate how their concrete actions on a day-to-day basis serve to meet those human needs.

When needs are met, when employees are getting what they want from their supervisors and their organization, they are more satisfied and more likely to remain in that motivational environment.

Current research confirms these same findings. Perry Pascarella in his book, *The New Achievers*, describes motivation of today's employees with the same facts. Pascarella insists that there is no lack of work ethic in America. Workers *do* want to make a lasting contribution, but they are prevented from doing so by American organizations and their managers.

To keep good people, and to keep them productive, corporate leaders need to carefully examine the impact of their organizational structure, philosophy, policies, and procedures. These critical aspects significantly influence the corporate culture which governs both attitudes and actions. These essential concerns are deliberately covered in the *first* chapter of the strategy section of this book.

Other current literature supports the importance of being attentive to the needs of employees. John Naisbitt and Patricia Aburdeen, co-authors of *Reinventing The Corporation*, look with more depth at current trends and the current predicament. Drawing the same conclusions, they emphasize that the companies who provide for the wants of their employees will attract and keep good people: productive people committed to making lasting, valuable contributions.

The authors describe these companies as *The Fortunate 500* with good reason.

Supervisors and managers are likely to be motivated by different priorities than front line operations employees. They have different perspectives and a driven by different needs. The same could apply to people like research and development employees. While the Maslow hierarchy is probably our best model to understand human wants and needs, we must be sensitive to differences among groups of employees and among individual members of our team.

To illustrate this, compare the results shown in the chart on page 41 with the following presentation of results of another study. The chart below illustrates the weights given to the same categories by over 300 first-level and second-level supervisors in one organization over a three year period. Note the similarities and differences, remembering that each factor is a potential motivator.

Motivational Factor	What First-Line Supervisors Say They Want	What Second-Line Supervisors Say They Want
good working conditions	6	6
feeling involvement in job	8	7
tactful disciplining	9	9
feedback on work well done	4	4
loyalty of supervisor	7	8
high wages (salary)	2	1
promotion and growth	3	3
help on personal problems	10	10
job security	5	5
interesting work	1	2

The marketplace is driving a renewed interest in productivity and quality. The economy is shifting away from an operations-intensive orientation in which quantitative concerns have a high value. In today's competitive environment, the new emphasis is on *quality*. The quality job has to be done by caring employees. The burden rests on the shoulders of the relatively few really good people on whom we can depend.

Now, more than ever, we need to reach those exceptional people, motivate them, and hold on to them. At the same time, we must build the same attitude and performance in our other employees with high potential. We can only do this if we know what they want from employers and managers, and if we manage in ways that will fulfill those wants.

This discussion could go on and on. But more examples would just take up space in this book and usurp your reading time. The essence of keeping good people is not in mere understanding, but in taking strategic action to make a positive difference.

Keeping Good People

SECTION TWO

Chapter 5

Strategic Responses

A recent study by Robert Half International, Inc., examined why people leave their jobs for supposedly greener pastures. The results of the study verified that compensation is not a predominant reason for change in employment.

Instead, people shift their loyalties to a new employer because of other, non-monetary factors. I emphasize this, because I have heard a great number of business owners, executives, managers, and supervisors express their belief that people "go where the money is." That simply isn't totally true anymore.

People are hungry for opportunities to grow in their jobs. They crave advancement, both in position and stature, and in responsibility and opportunity. If they can't find avenues for growth in one environment, they'll seek them in another.

Please Notice Me!

Human beings want attention and recognition. We get so little attention from others, we're really hungry for any kind of acknowledgment of our value (or even our existence).

Think about the reception you got when you went home last night. Remember how your spouse greeted you enthusiastically at the door? Remember how you were asked about how things went at work? And the genuine concern for the projects you're involved in? Did your solicitous spouse invite you to join in the preparation of your family meal--let's do it together?

As you crossed the threshold, did your kids turn off the television with excited exclamations about your arrival? Did they come bounding over, eager to tell you about their adventures at school? And did your dog leap off the hearth to share affection at your feet, tail wagging vigorously with expressive yelps punctuating the expressions of delight that you were home?

Maybe the dog sounds familiar, but the rest must have been at someone else's house? Welcome to the real world! Few of us get the attention we'd like at home. So, we look elsewhere for satisfaction of the basic human need to be appreciated and cared about.

Wouldn't it be nice if we could experience that kind of attention at work? After all, we spend more of our waking hours at work than we do at home anyway. Research shows that people often leave an employer because they haven't received the recognition they want.

As a interesting side comment, we can learn a lot by watching children. Ever notice how a child responds to positive attention? If children can't get positive attention from adults, parents and teachers, they deliberately misbehave to earn some kind of attention. Adults are just kids grown up.

Managers Set the Course

While peer "pressures" and norms guide the way many people behave and think in the work environment, let's recognize that managers have a significant influence on the attitudes of their employees. The way people are treated by their managers--several layers up, not just their immediate superior--will determine their satisfaction, productivity, and longevity.

It is unrealistic to think that people will be happy with everything management decides or does. Camelot doesn't really exist. Reality is that some people will differ with management from time to time. This is expected by mature people in any organization. Often the key is not *what* is done, but *how* it is done...and explained.

People want to be treated with respect. They want to be seen as being important to the organization's success, and recognized for their parts in making positive things happen. When people issues are well addressed by management, employees will demonstrate their loyalty and dedication as team players under the most adverse circumstances. However, when people are not treated well, they won't "invest" themselves in the company even under the best of corporate circumstances.

Managers have to consciously and deliberately work with their people to get things done. The way they apply the principles presented in this and other books on leadership and management will determine their success in building stable, productive teams.

Enlightened employers who want to be successful in the 1990s will emphasize to their managers and supervisors the value of being people-oriented. Every indication we see points to the critical importance of building genuine, positive relationships with people--employees, customers, and suppliers.

Strategic Leadership

The "meat" of this book is an abundance of things that organization leaders can do to keep good people as productive members of their team. The application of these approaches is done strategically, hence the description of these techniques as "strategies".

To do something strategically means to plan in advance, as opposed to responding to emergent conditions with a knee-jerk reaction. Certainly, there will be those times when a fast response is needed to keep a valued employee. However, the premise of this book is that those times will be infrequent if the recommended strategies are applied.

Please note that strategies (plural) need to be applied. You can not simply apply one strategy and assume that all your people will be loyal and productive forever! A variety of strategies have to be applied, with constant attention to how they are received by your people. Expect to do some fine tuning, since each situation is different and each individual's needs will be different.

Our emphasis is on having people be productive members of our team. We want them to achieve results, enabling the entire organization to achieve its objectives and maintain its existence with continual accomplishment of goals.

Before people can be productive, they have to know what is expected of them. Before they can be members of a team, there has to be a conscious team. And teams need leaders. Those team leaders do things, strategically and carefully, to build the team and empower members to "win"...individually and collectively.

Your task, as leader, is to apply the various strategies in this book in a deliberate fashion to meet those objectives. Some strategies will be applied uniformly, with all people treated the same way. Others will be applied on an individual level, meeting personal needs.

This differential treatment is quite legitimate, although we sometimes try to hide it behind insistence that we treat everyone equally. As a good leader, you should not try to treat everyone equally; instead, focus on treating them each *fairly*. Today, more than ever, we are leading a workforce comprised of individuals. It is critical that we don't ignore their individual characteristics.

The strategies presented on the following pages are interdependent. They can easily be applied on their own, without any consideration of any other strategy. They can be strengthened by combination with another strategy. You can mix and match as you wish. There is no pre-determined formula.

The collection of strategies in this book should not be considered to be complete. It represents the author's best efforts at time of publication. As you discover other strategies, by talking with fellow leaders, reading books or articles, or by trial and error, I'd be interested in learning about them. If enough new strategies are brought to my attention, a second edition of the book is a strong possibility.

Don't be limited by what you read in these pages. Stay alert for other ideas. Keep learning! Record your new knowledge in the space available in this book so *Keeping Good People* may serve as a living reference for you for years to come.

Chapter 6

Environmental Strategies

The primary strategies for keeping good people, and keeping them productive, deal with the working environment. "Environment" today means much more than it has in the past. We look at a much bigger picture than we ever have before.

The environmental strategies address three crucial aspects of the workplace:
1. the ethics and values foundation on which the organization is built
2. the policies that interpret those values and translate them into operative action
3. the physical environment that is a concrete manifestation of the organization's concern for the space that its people occupy.

While seemingly different, these strategies are all linked by the common thread of their impact on the human behavior that shapes what the organization is...and can become.

The ethics and values establish the organization's character, its moral fiber. These strategies determine how decisions will be made, how people will be treated and how they will treat others, and how business will be conducted. Ethics and values create and confirm the organization's place in our Society.

The American public is focusing more intently on ethics issues. We see evidence of this attitude and concern in the way we respond when cheating is uncovered. It doesn't even require that we be the victim. If our sense of right and wrong, of fair play, is violated, we become angry.

Our most obvious examples, thanks to news coverage, are the episodes involving inappropriate purchases by the federal government. Outrageous prices for things like hammers and toilet seats enrage the public, and rightly so. We expect a different kind of behavior from our public officials as well as those private sector vendors who deal with them.

Policies are designed based on the organization's ethics and values. Our policies give us living guidelines regarding the way we function. Values and policies are so intertwined, it is hard to separate them in many cases. And it should be that way.

We determine our policies, in a wide range of areas, to legitimize what we do. They often clearly deliniate what we will not do. Following the policies, we move forward in our leadership well-grounded in the organization's values-based stance and direction.

The physical place in which people work says a lot about the organization, its values, and its policies. The more comfortable the place is, as a work environment, the more productive will be those who work there. Satisfaction and contentment with surroundings greatly influence the way people work and their interest in remaining with the employer.

All these elements bond together to establish and maintain the feeling your people have about their work environment.

Let's look at the ethics and values and policy strategies to keep good people:

Ethics, Values, and Policies

The successful companies of the future, let alone the present, will be based on solid ethical principles. Corporate values will be recognized as the vital lifeblood that pulls people together and keeps them together.

Dealing with these matters will be difficult for some companies and their management teams. Until recently such concerns have not been important enough, sensitive enough, to address directly. Now they are becoming decision points for current and prospective employees, for customers, and even for suppliers.

A company's reputation rests on more than just the quality of its products, although that is one important value. Insiders and outsiders judge companies by their philosophy and level of customer service, their involvement in community activities, and their commitment to moral, environmental, and even political issues. Corporate management has dealt with these concerns in the past, but usually not to the extent of having defined official policies and positions.

Our changing expectations of the employers' role and responsibility in the American Scene is "forcing" companies to examine carefully the way the organization functions. The companies are judged by where they operate their business, as seen by the reaction to companies with facilities in South Africa. They are even judged by the content of the television shows they sponsor.

Today's employees, particularly, are becoming more concerned about moral and ethical issues in business. The corporation's values, as expressed in company statements, in annual reports, and in daily operative behavior, affect how people feel about remaining with an employer. Workers want to be comfortable with what their employer stands for. They seek compatibility of those corporate positions with their own personal viewpoints.

When good employees, aware of social issues, sense a strong divergence between their value positions and those of their employer, the likelihood of their divorcing themselves from the employer is greater than ever before in our history. Never before has such a high level of values consciousness been combined with a high level of alternative employment opportunities. The result is an understandably volatile situation.

With the seriousness of these concerns in mind, let's consider some values and ethics strategies for keeping good people.

Strategy 6.1
Share a common vision.

The chances of success are much greater for your organization if you have a clearly defined vision that all your people can follow. We call this written version of the vision a mission statement or statement of purpose. This definition serves as the foundation, the common thread, for everything the organization does.

Your statement should be succinct. It should fit comfortably on one page, typed double-spaced or typeset. Explain why you are in business. Validate the reason for your company even existing, and specify the kind(s) of business you're in. Include any foundation beliefs that guide your decisions. For example, some of our clients state that they operate "according to Christian principles."

Express the value you place on your employees, your customers, your suppliers, and your stockholders. How do you treat them?

Where will your entity go in the future? Is the mission to grow? To remain the same size, providing increasingly good products and services to a fixed geographic or demographic market? Will you diversify or limit the areas in which you are involved? How will the organization look in the future?

In developing your statement, I urge you to make the process a team effort. Involve managers from various levels of the corporate hierarchy. Bring non-managerial employees into the picture. Solicit input from your board of directors. Not only will you benefit from several perspectives, you will have the opportunity to cross-check the legitimacy of each element of your statement.

An important advantage of involving a number of key people is that people support what they help to create. Your mission statement is worthless if every member of your team doesn't support it. Discuss the concepts. Gain agreement on what you're really all about. Choose your words carefully and shape your sentences deliberately to say what you want to say.

Once you have an acceptable mission statement, begin putting it to work. This is a valuable tool for you to assure that everyone believes what's being said. The first step is to spread the word. Show all your employees what has been developed. Some companies share the draft statement with employees, offering opportunities for review and comment before the document is finalized.

When the Mission Statement is finished and approved by everyone who has to approve it, begin making it a part of your corporate culture. You do this by introducing it to all your employees with an explanation of what it means to the company and to each employee. Next, introduce your new Mission Statement to your customers, suppliers, job applicants, and anyone else doing business with your organization. Here are some suggestions to consider:

• Post the Mission Statement on bulletin boards in your facility, where it will be seen by employees and visitors.

• Put framed copies of the Mission Statement in the offices of all executives, managers, and supervisors. The frames can be hung on the wall or placed on desks, credenzas, filing cabinets, or tables.

• Place framed copies on the walls in offices, employee lounges, near coffee machines or water coolers, and other places where employees will see it.

• Enclose copies in payroll envelopes so each employee receives a personal copy.

• Give copies to customers during sales calls. As appropriate, send copies to customers. Enclose a copy in each shipment of merchandise.

• Post your Mission Statement in the purchasing department and give copies to the salespeople calling on your company. Let them know what you stand for, what you believe. Place emphasis on purchasing ethics: no bribes, kickbacks, or other unethical practices will be tolerated.

• Display a copy on the wall of the personnel office. Give a copy, or show one, to each applicant. Explain what the Mission Statement means, especially as it applies to the company's expectations of its employees and what the company sees as its obligations/responsibilities to its employees.

To reinforce the concepts and importance of your company's mission statement, you might schedule periodic meetings of all employees, or groups of employees. During these sessions, discuss the meaning and relevance of the Mission Statement and how it is applied in the daily work of the organization.

Make your mission statement real, legitimate, and permanent.

Strategy 6.2
Value each individual.

Each of your people is an individual human being. Each of those individuals is unique and special.

Value each person for who and what he or she is. Recognize what each person can become. Appreciate the contribution each person makes to the organization and to fellow team members.

While working with your people as a group, never forget that each of those people is an individual. They see themselves as part of the team, as part of your organization. But, even more importantly, they see themselves as an individual and should be respected and treated that way.

Strategy 6.3
Work together as a team.

The people who work for an employer are individuals. They apply their personal talents, knowledge, abilities, and energy to accomplish the work of the organization. People can do this strictly as individuals, or as members of a team.

The choice, to function independently or as part of a team, is made consciously. The impact of the choice is the attitude the employee will have about his/her relationship with the employer and with fellow employees. The more the employee interacts with other members of the team, the greater will be the bonds linking the employee with the organization.

When people work together in teams, they get more accomplished, both in qualitative and quantitative terms. While there are tasks that are best done on an individual basis, most work benefits from the involvement of more than one person's effort.

Whether people work alone or in teams is a consequence of the operating philosophy of the organization. This philosophy is established and maintained by senior management, but is also strongly influenced by middle managers and supervisors. By your actions, by the way you assign work and lead, you determine how much and how well people will work together.

To build an organizational climate that encourages people to work together, emphasize the value of working together as a team. Encourage cooperation, collaboration, networking, sharing, and camaraderie. Assign tasks or projects to groups, or suggest that individuals accepting assignments call upon others to assist them.

Teamwork involves a common striving for goals and objectives that are understood and agreed-to by all concerned. In your leadership role, strive to clarify those goals and objectives with your people. Initiate discussions that serve to build consensus in work groups and in the organization as a whole.

Effective teamwork involves members communicating with each other, assuring that everyone has access to needed information. Beyond access, teamwork implies a more active communications flow enabling all members to know what others are doing, why they are doing it, and what they will do in the future. It's a deliberate, assertive process.

You can make it easier for people to work in teams. Support the team concept by facilitating teamwork interaction. For example, provide work areas that are more conducive to team operation. Place people in reasonable proximity to each other; make it easier for them to work with others. This includes giving people enough space to be together as they work on joint projects. Don't expect people to work well as teams if their work area consists of small one-person cubicles with no common areas. Don't expect close cooperation and collaboration among people at opposite ends of a plant or in separate buildings.

To enable your people to work better in teams, give them ways to communicate with each other. A place to meet is a good first step, but team functioning is also enhanced by the use of communications technology such as good telephone systems and networked personal computers. Facsimile machines, conference call equipment, and other technologies still being developed, enhance the ability of people to communicate in a quick, efficient manner.

Stay alert for any opportunity to reinforce the value and importance of people working together for the common good of the organization. Do whatever you can to support and strengthen people's capacity to function as a team.

Strategy 6.4
Loyalty is a two-way relationship.

To keep your good people, you naturally want your employees to feel strong bonds of loyalty to the organization. If you treat your employees well, following the philosophy expressed through the strategies in this book, the feelings of loyalty will be there.

Loyalty is a two-way relationship. If you expect your people to be loyal to you, you have to be loyal to them. Being loyal to your employees means avoiding layoffs as much as possible. It means backing them up when they need help in dealing with a customer or supplier. Loyalty to employees includes understanding when someone makes an honest mistake, not terminating them or applying severe discipline when an employee's error or accident was unintentional.

Loyalty means giving them appropriate support in their personal lives when they are in trouble. This kind of support is most often given through employee assistance programs offering confidential service from mental health counselors, alcoholism clinics, legal specialists, and similar professionals. A number of employers will grant pay advances or special leaves of absence to help their valued employees over the rough road of life.

Some companies show their loyalty by making company equipment or facilities available for employee use on personal time. As an example, many companies that have trucks will allow employees to use them on their own time to move furniture, dirt, or something else appropriate for the vehicle. Others will make shop tools available for employees to take home to work on personal projects. If your company values suggest supporting your people in such ways, be sure your corporate policy is clear to avoid misunderstandings. It's wise to be sure your insurance policies cover you and your people, too.

Do those extra things to demonstrate your loyalty to your people, and they will do extra things to show their loyalty to you.

Strategy 6.5
Enthusiasm is justified and appropriate.

If you have reason to be enthusiastic about your people, your organization, your potential, and your success, show it! If pride and enthusiasm and team spirit is justified, support the expression of these feelings as a company. Make this kind of positive communication a shared value as part of your corporate culture.

When people operate as a team, and achieve success, they should be able to celebrate their wins. If such celebrations are suppressed or prohibited, it dampens the motivation to work as hard for the victories.

Enthusiasm can be experienced at the time of winning and also while the race is being run. Build positive feelings among your people toward what you are doing. Emphasize how each person is contributing toward your organization's achievement. Stay excited!

Strategy 6.6
We are all here for the customer.

The successful companies, today and into the future, will be those that are customer-driven. If you want to be competitive, on the leading edge of your industry, include deliberate high-level customer service as one of your company's principal values.

Building the most effective kind of attitude toward customer service will not come just from training people to smile and say, "Thank you for shopping at ...." Your attitude toward customers must be a deliberate strategy flowing from the very top of your organization.

This is another one of those aspects, like most of the values we're discussing, where actions speak louder than words. All your people will be watching to see how senior management regards customer service. The employees on the front lines, interacting directly with your customers, will perform as they see their leaders performing.

If management treats employees well, there's a pretty good chance the employees will treat the customers well. If management treats employees badly, expect the same kind of treatment to be extended to customers. There's a moral here.

To facilitate good customer service, give careful consideration to the design of your policies that affect the way your people can deal with customers. Examine all your policies that impact on customer service. Begin with pricing, then look at the range of flexibility your salespeople have.

Does your paperwork requirement support or frustrate the efforts of your people to serve your customers? How much do your policies enable or hamper your service staff and customer relations specialists as they seek to resolve the problems that always arise?

Some of the most successful companies in the customer service arena give their employees a considerable amount of authority to make things "right" for the customer. Some restaurants give not only managers, but servers, the authority to discount prices, give meals away, or give gift certificates when striving to satisfy a disgruntled customer. Clerks in retail stores have freedom to accept returned merchandise without receipts. Manufacturers' customer service representatives can replace parts or products at no charge to the customer to "make it right."

Giving front-line people such power strengthens their ability to respond to the customer's needs. Feeling the company's sincere desire to do business the right way inspires customers to return to continue doing business with such companies. This becomes a driving force and a source of pride for the employees who care about the company and the customer. The result is a win-win-win relationship.

Some employees will half-apologetically confess that they don't serve customers. Folks in positions in accounting, computer systems, or manufacturing often don't relate to the company's customers. Help them appreciate the impact they have on the company's success through serving their customers in the other departments of the company. Everyone in the organization serves the company's customer, directly or indirectly.

Strategy 6.7
Have a set of Guiding Principles.

This strategy is a partner to Strategy 6.1. The common vision of the organization, expressed as a mission statement, defines what you are and where you are going. The principles address some of the underlying values that guide you along that path of corporate progress.

A number of companies invest some time to define the principles by which the organization operates. These are usually a reflection of the principles adhered to by owners and/or senior management. After all, as we've discussed, these key people set the pace for everyone else.

The principles indicate attitudes and approaches to dealing with others. They form the criteria guiding how decisions will be made. Principles include such categories as honesty and integrity, ethics, orientation toward religious foundations, long-term relationships versus brief encounters, and being self-serving as opposed to other-serving, and fair treatment for all. Issues such as health and safety can be addressed, perhaps determining whether you will have a non- smoking environment, pre-employment and/or annual physical examinations, and enforcement of safety measures such as wearing earplugs and safety glasses.

The clearer you make your guiding principles, and the more they are consciously used in making decisions, the more they will become a part of your operating philosophy. After people understand your principles, they won't need to ask for your value judgment on a matter before they are able to consider it and make the appropriate decision on their own.

It's usually very helpful to establish and maintain a clear list of guiding principles to help each person in a management position. When they understand your philosophical approach, it will be easier for them to make decisions on their own. This will give management people more time to focus on the external business of the organization.

Strategy 6.8
Offer stability, security, risk, as needed.

You can influence worker productivity and job satisfaction by the degree of stability and risk you offer. Although the terms sound opposite, both can be comfortably present in the same organizational environment.

The concept of risk usually goes hand-in-hand with change. Organizational change has become a fact of life. The three constants in our lives are death, taxes, and change. The problem with change, from the perspectives of many people, is the disruption of stability. When stability is shaken, fears of damage to security follow close behind.

Change is necessary in organizations. Without change, leading toward positive progress, organizations slide backward. The loss is either directly measurable or is relative to the competition. However you judge your position, it is clear that you must deliberately move forward to survive and thrive. Change is a necessity.

If the organization offers a foundation of stability, change comes more easily. In a stable organization, the risks associated with change are more comfortable because of the sense of security felt by members of the organization. If you want to encourage positive change with minimal or at least calculated risk, take steps to maintain the stability of your organization to support the change.

These concepts are mutually supportive. Stability and security are enhanced by the organization taking the risks to make changes and try new approaches to stay on the cutting edge. The more your people are "on the edge" in a positive way, the greater will be the excitement about making progress and staying "on top" of any situation. (See Strategy 7.30.)

Organizations that strive for too much stability tend to resist change, growth, and responsiveness. Those that aim for too much risk may endanger their own security by exposing vulnerability. Your greatest success will come from striking a reasonable balance between stability and risk to provide long-term security.

Strategy 6.9
Prohibit discrimination of any kind.

Since the Civil Rights Act of 1964, we have become legally and morally sensitive to preventing discrimination. Beyond the legal implications, discrimination may inhibit your opportunities to gain the high potential of contributions and longevity of employment by those who may be targets for discrimination. If your good people believe they are being discriminated against, whether it is true or not, they will probably leave you for a more accepting environment.

Traditionally, we do not permit discrimination on the basis of race, creed, color, national origin, religion, sex, or age. These areas of difference are covered by federal law, so they are violated only at great risk.

There are other areas of difference that could serve as a basis for discrimination, perhaps causing you to lose some of your best people. Even though, as human beings, people have prejudices, guard against discrimination in employment based on such factors as:
- level of education
- use of grammar in spoken or written communication
- home state (examples: people in Ohio often put down those from West Virginia. Indiana residents harbor similar feeling for folks from Kentucky.)

- style of dress or other appearance factors including hair style, body weight or height, and skin blemishes
- regional accents
- neighborhood of residence
- type of vehicle owned
- marital or parental status
- sports activity
- political party identification
- use of tobacco products: cigarettes, cigars, pipes, chewing tobacco
- relationship preferences.

The list can go on and on. And, yes, managers and entire organizations still discriminate for or against employees or potential employees based on these criteria. Be wary that you aren't scaring away, or blatantly sending away, some of your best talent because of such short-sightedness.

When you discover discrimination, take immediate and definitive steps to negate the discrimination and clarify for all concerned that such discrimination will not be tolerated.

Strategy 6.10
Eschew profanity.

Now, there's an interesting word we don't see every day. Eschew. For years I saw that word in an expression, "eschew obfuscation," and wondered what it meant. Finally, when I grew mature enough to stop resisting my parents' insistence that I look things up in the dictionary, I discovered the meaning of the confusing words and phrase.

Eschew means to shun or avoid. Obfuscation is making things unclear or obscure. Thus, I discovered, that hard-to-comprehend phrase demonstrated very plainly to make things clear.

Eschew seems like a good word to attach to profanity in the workplace. Shun it. Avoid it. Profanity is totally inappropriate for people in management or other influential positions. Don't use it on a regular basis, as part of your normal vocabulary; and try to find alternative words when you are angry or frustrated. Yes, I know "fudge" doesn't seem to be as satisfying, but think of the people around you.

A lot of people, even in today's more liberal times, don't like cursing. Being around someone who curses is uncomfortable for them. They find it difficult to respect someone using profanity. It can be particularly distasteful if they don't use those kinds of words at all themselves. They may never say anything to you, but the feelings are there anyway.

Even those people who use profanity themselves, on a regular basis or on "special occasions," have less respect for others who use it. This especially applies to their attitudes toward people in leadership positions. It lowers their opinion of you.

Appreciate that people follow your lead. If you curse, expect them to do the same. If cursing is accepted on an employee-to-employee basis, it won't be long before cursing will be easy to do in front of the customers...and then to the customers. On a recent trip, I stopped at a drug store for some cold medicine. Imagine my feelings when the pharmacist, helping me make my selection, used profanity in our conversation.

What do your personal and organizational values believe about profanity? Can you legitimately establish a policy, and adhere to it yourself?

Strategy 6.11
Be fair and honest.

It almost seems insulting to include this as an environmental strategy for your consideration. But, it is something that must be addressed when constructing your overall statement of organizational values.

Do your people understand clearly the organization's position on fairness and honesty? You might be surprised. This is another of those things where what you do speaks louder than what you say.

If you're going to be fair and honest, those standards must be applied in all dealings with employees, customers, unions, suppliers, and the community. If you are not honest in your dealings with suppliers, don't expect your employees to believe you'll be honest with them.

If you expect your people to be fair and honest with others, including each other and you, set the example. Otherwise, you may end up like the drug-abusing father who couldn't understand why his kids "turned bad." Your people at work watch you just as much as your children do at home. And vice versa.

Strategy 6.12
Facilitate a family feeling.

Some business owners and managers shy away from the idea of having a family feeling among their employees. They believe that a business is just that, a business. A family is different.

A family feeling does not mean you're giving away the store. It does mean that people can call each other by their first names or nicknames. More formal terms of address can be used when company's there, like a client, but the feeling of comfort with each other is present.

In a family, people care about each other. While they are bonded together, they are also free to be individuals. They hold a strong allegiance to each other, defending that togetherness against outsiders. They share responsibilities.

Family members also squabble from time to time. Differences are brought out relatively quickly, dealt with in direct and sometimes emotional ways, then put to rest. Parent-child relationships are productive.

There are many positive aspects to our sense of family in our cultures. Even the negative aspects have their positive attributes. If applied properly, the family feeling can be very healthy for any organization.

Strategy 6.13
Value professional standing.

Many professions, and some trades, have requirements for certain levels of education, experience, qualification, and continuing education. These elements of professional membership and designation are important to those in the professions. They should also be of value to the organizations employing those people.

If you want to attract and hold professionals, demonstrate that you value their status and respect their credentials. The respect and appreciation will be returned. Disdain the professional standing, and you will "force" some of your key people to seek positions where their professionalism is recognized.

There are a number of ways that professional standings can be recognized. Let's consider some:

● Encourage framing and posting of certificates affirming educational achievement and professional designation. Call attention to those credentials when taking visitor on tours of your facilities.

● If members of your team hold professional designations authorizing the use of identifying initials after their name, encourage the employee to use the designation in correspondence and when his/her name is shown on reports, proposals, and official documents.

- Support participation in professional organizations, including granting time to attend meetings or conventions of those in the profession. Many companies pay the dues for their employees to facilitate their involvement in their profession.
- Recognize the status of your people in annual reports, newspaper or magazine or newsletter articles, stockholder reports, and other publications. When professional accomplishments are made, publicize them proudly.
- Pay for subscriptions to professional journals so your people can keep current in their fields.
- Whenever appropriate, call upon your professionals for their expertise in solving problems or looking at alternatives.

Strategy 6.14
Promote integrity.

State and re-state your desire for honesty and honor in the behavior of all members of your organization. Emphasize the high value you place on righteousness, and refusal to compromise personal or corporate values.

Abide by a code of ethics in your organization. Clarify your expectation that everyone will follow that same code, with termination being a probable consequence for violating that trust. (*See Strategy 6.7.*)

No more needs to be said. Either you have it or you don't.

Strategy 6.15
Encourage camaraderie.

Camaraderie refers to companionship. It's a fellowship, an enjoyment of being with each other, enjoying each other's company. The feeling is one of being pals, almost best of friends. It's a closeness that says we enjoy being with each other.

In the business world, we can encourage people to build relationships with each other. Going out to lunch together, working on projects together, joining colleagues or coworkers in bowling leagues, golf outings, family picnics, and car pooling all strengthen the bonds of camaraderie.

People who enjoy one another are usually more productive in the workplace. They have greater loyalty to each other and to the organization which makes it possible for them to be together, to work together for common good.

Strategy 6.16
Promote a healthy working environment.

If you care about your people, you'll want them to have a healthy working environment. You can help create it and promote it.

Assure good engineering of heating, air conditioning, and ventilating systems. Maintain a healthy environment in which people can work. (*See Strategy 6.43 for additional discussion of this.*)

In areas that are not conducive to clean air, such as those that are in certain production facilities, provide breathing masks and "clean" rooms where workers can take a break. In "the old days," the emphasis was on getting the work out. Little, if any, care was given to the impact of the production environment on the health of the employees. Today we still must have the same concerns for production, but certainly not at the expense of the workers.

An increasing number of employers are establishing smoke-free environments in the workplace. In some cases, an entire facility is declared smoke-free. This may place a hardship on employees with a smoking habit. Employers are using the resources available from various health organizations to help people stop smoking. Some even offer cash bonuses for employees who quit smoking, payable after they have not smoked for some period of time.

For health, safety, and legal reasons, employers also ban alcohol and drugs from the workplace. If employees come to work under the influence of alcohol or drugs, they are sent home. Coming to work under the influence is an offense punishable by discharge in many companies.

If this is a value in your company, enforce it among all your employees. Include executives who may now indulge in the so-called three martini lunch. Include managers who may keep a bottle in their desk drawer for special occasions. Include salesmen who have cocktails when taking customers out to lunch. You may want to join those companies that simply don't reimburse liquor purchases on expense accounts.

To promote health, consider establishing a wellness program for your employees. Such educational and support programs can range from making health literature available to educational seminars to full-blown organized exercise regimen.

Professional assistance is available to help you design and implement any kind of wellness program you want. Check with resources such as:
- the outreach people at your community's hospital
- registered dieticians who practice in your area
- training professionals who have wellness courses
- health clubs, exercise centers, and sports medicine clinics
- recreation departments operated by municipal governments
- local school systems.

If the kind of program you are seeking does not exist, your chances are pretty good that one or more of the listed resources will be glad to help you put something together. You don't have to be elaborate or spend a lot of money to promote good health among your employees and their families.

Strategy 6.17
Insist on workplace safety.

This is another one of those strategies that should go without saying. However, to be sure it is not overlooked, let's talk a few minutes about safety.

As the expression goes, "safety is everybody's business." We practically take it for granted that employers want a safe environment, as do their employees. Sometimes taking things for granted is foolish. This is one of those times.

Safety needs to be demanded and emphasized from the top of the organization. Those senior executives responsible must also get out of their offices and go out to where people are working to assure safety measures are implemented. Enforcement by the federal Occupational Health and Safety Administration (OSHA) is not as strong as it used to be; enforcement is now up to the employer. And employers are legally and morally liable when accidents occur.

In the past few months, I have personally been in several manufacturing plants where senior management insists that safety is a paramount concern. In one company, when we toured the production area we counted almost two dozen obvious safety hazards. How many did we overlook because we are not trained safety engineers? In the other plant, we saw employees working without their required safety glasses and ear protectors.

It's not enough to say safety is important. The message must be conveyed clearly to front line supervisors. Those supervisors, and their hourly subordinates, must have the authority, responsibility, and accountability to correct safety problems before someone gets hurt. It's perfectly legitimate to place the burden of accountability on front line supervisors.

Supervisors are traditionally caught in the middle, trying to satisfy all the demands made upon them by management, employees, and customers, without having to contend with additional duties or extra work dumped on them by outsiders. If you insist that a supervisor keep the work area clean and safe, you may get an angry question in response: which is more important: getting the work out on time, or having a clean, safe work area? How you answer determines the value that will be placed on health and safety.

To emphasize safety, employers will erect signs showing how many days have passed since the last lost-time accident. The space where the number of days is shown is painted so chalk can be used to change the number of days each evening or morning. Other signs use cards with numbers and holes so they can be hung on hooks. Hopefully, changing numbers will be a long-time ritual.

Safety dinners are held throughout the country. Employees wear shirts proclaiming the company's safety record. Awards are given for safe operation. For more ideas and support materials for an ongoing safety campaign, contact the National Safety Council, 444 North Michigan Avenue, Chicago 60611. Their telephone number is (312) 527-4800.

Strategy 6.18
Avoid stupid rules.

Every organization needs rules to guide its operation. The writing and enforcement of these rules is an obligation of management. Naturally, the company would expect the rules to be followed.

If you institute stupid rules that are not needed, that conflict with the corporate culture or with other rules, or that just don't make any sense, your people will have a negative attitude toward all rules. The disdain for the silly rules easily carries over to apply to all rules.

Simple solution: make sure that any rules, regulations, policies, procedures, and operating methods are reasonable and appropriate. They should always support the efforts of the organization and team members to get the job done.

Herman's Law of Rule Making says: as organizations grow larger, there is a tendency to make more rules. Even if everything was running just fine, an increase in the number of employees or locations seems to generate a proportional increase in the number of rules. Rules are necessary for some situations. Concentrate on those and ignore the other issues.

Guard against the propensity to create more and more rules in bureaucratic organizations. Cut through red tape; don't create more! Red tape is not biodegradable, so it is not healthy for the earth's environment.

(*See Strategy 8.7 for a further discussion on the role of "Mickey Mouse" in the workplace.*)

Strategy 6.19
Provide flexibility in working hours.

With family and personal needs, some of your employees and potential employees may have some difficulty with traditional working hours. To attract and keep your good people, be sensitive to personal needs and make the adjustments you can.

As an employer, you have a number of alternatives. Consider what is best for the employee and the company; seek those win-win solutions.

One alternative is to institute flex-time in your organization. This arrangement gives people freedom to choose their own working hours, as long as they work eight hours a day or forty hours a week. There are variations to this approach, but essentially you set the parameters and your people work within them.

Let's look at the eight hour day approach. If your official working hours are 9:00 a.m. to 5:00 p.m., you may require that at least six hours of an employee's work day fall between those hours. This gives the employee freedom to work from 7:00 a.m. to 3:00 p.m., from 11:00 a.m. to 7:00 p.m., or any eight hour schedule in between.

On the forty hour week approach, employees design their own schedule of how and when they will work the forty hours. They may choose to work four ten-hour days. They may work four nine-hour days and one four-hour day. There are a lot of variations on the theme. Teams of employees negotiate their schedules so the facility is adequately staffed from 9:00 to 5:00, or whatever your core hours may be.

Not all jobs will lend themselves to this kind of flexibility in working hours. Be careful to establish clear guidelines before beginning a flex-time program. Initiate it as an experiment, subject to termination if things don't work out.

Another alternative is to allow people to vary the hours they work based on child care needs. Many working mothers would like to start their work day right after the children leave for school. By the time the children return home, Mom wants to be there to greet her offspring. Many of your jobs will allow that kind of flexibility, especially in the office environment. You may find that some production lines can be scheduled with the same kinds of considerations.

More and more employers are allowing their people to do all or part of their work at home. With developing technology, such as modems that link computers located at home and office, facsimile machines, and conference call mechanisms, the possibilities are endless.

An increasing number of women are earning college degrees and going to work in responsible positions. As their careers begin developing, these valuable employees may want to have one or more children. You can keep them on your team by giving them a non-paid leave to give birth and care for the child for a reasonable period of time. When they are ready to return to work, welcome them back and enable them to continue along their established career path. Be receptive to men wanting to take some time off during childbirth and infancy time.

Some valuable employees with a high social consciousness may want to invest part of their lives in missionary work or community service. Others may be involved with the National Guard or military Reserves. Support these people by giving them flexibility to pursue their own interests and they will demonstrate their loyalty to you by returning even stronger than when they departed.

Establish a company policy regarding the length of time you will hold a job or opportunity open, how you will handle benefits and benefit eligibility (check with your carrier), and whether you will pay the employee during absence from the job. Even if you give yourself some flexibility in your guidelines, set the policy and stick with it. This will help your employees understand your position and will eliminate confusion later.

Strategy 6.20
Apply progressive discipline fairly.

There are two parts to this strategy. One is to apply progressive discipline. The other is to apply it fairly.

Progressive discipline means following a series of deliberate steps in disciplining an employee for infractions of company rules. By following these steps, you are fair to the employee, you avoid capricious actions, and your disciplinary process will stand up in court.

The steps of progressive discipline increase in seriousness and intensity as you proceed with the enforcement procedure:

1. The first step is informational. During this initial phase, make sure the employee fully understands what is expected in terms of behavior and performance. Applying this step will solve most problems that arise from unclear expectations.

2. If the problem persists, the second step is to initiate the formal discipline process with the verbal warning, or verbal reprimand. In this interview, the superior informs the errant employee of the expectations and specifically how the expectations are not being met. Agreement is reached as to how the employee can correct the problem.

The supervisor states that this is a verbal notification of dissatisfaction with the employee's performance. If the problem is not corrected, further discipline may result. (Use may instead of will to give yourself flexibility in the future. You might want to issue more than one verbal reprimand before moving to the next step.)

3. The third step is the written reprimand, or written warning. This is similar to the verbal reprimand, except that the communication is put in writing. The written memorandum includes a description of the behavior that is expected of the employee, then what the employee is perceived to be doing. Document that a written reprimand had been given, the date, and the employee's response at that time.

Next, write down how and when you expect the employee to correct the behavior or overcome the problem. If supervisory support will be needed to get things back on track, indicate what kind of support will be given--by whom, when, and how.

Again, include the statement that if the problem is not corrected, further disciplinary action may be taken. The employee gets a copy of the memorandum, and a copy goes into the employee's personnel file.

4. If the problem still persists, your next step is a suspension. This involves giving the employee time off without pay for anywhere from one to thirty days. Usually, one, two, or three days will convey the seriousness of your message. Again, state the expected behavior, the perceived behavior, what must be done to correct the problem, and the statement that additional disciplinary action may be taken.

Some companies are using a variation that involves a paid suspension. The employee is given time off with pay, but must return with a written plan for how the problem behavior will be corrected. Studies show that many employees treated this way either correct their behavior or resign.

5. The final step in the progressive discipline process is termination. If the other steps have not produced the desired results, it is usually necessary to discharge the employee. Again, this should be done in writing, stipulating the dates of the verbal reprimand, written reprimand, and suspension.

If all the steps have been followed, and the discipline is legitimate, the administrative or civil courts will probably support your position if the discharged employee appeals. If you do not follow and document the steps, you are open for criticism and possible reversal of your discharge.

Strategy 6.21
Make work fun.

People should enjoy their jobs. If people don't enjoy what they are doing, they should resign their positions and go find something they can enjoy.

Happy employees are more productive employees. They are comfortable in their work environment, so they remain in that environment for a longer period of time.

Your challenge is to create and maintain an environment where people can enjoy their work, can enjoy being a part of your team. There are a number of ways to do this, ranging from the way you decorate the work area (*see Strategy 6.38 and Strategy 6.44*) to the attitudes toward enjoying work.

Bring out the positive aspects of your team's environment. Celebrate the victories. Celebrate birthdays. Do some silly things once in a while just to have some fun. Be careful not to ridicule anyone or cause any damage in the process.

Laugh!

Don't turn the place into a country club or a comedy fair, but have fun. Bring in a pizza once in a while for lunch. Buy ice cream bars for everyone on a warm day. Hire some high school students to wash everyone's car while they work. These things will carry over to support positive attitudes that will reinforce work being fun...an enjoyable experience rather than an oppressive drudgery.

As the expression goes, "take what you do seriously, but don't take yourself too seriously."

Strategy 6.22
Celebrate achievements, birthdays, and other occasions.

Share the positive aspects of relationships among the people who are part of your organization's team. This doesn't mean a continual party, but does suggest that some time out is appropriate once in a while to celebrate. We've known for years that bonds among people, as well as people and organizations, are strengthened by celebration.

When individuals, or teams of individuals, or the organization as a whole, has achieved something worthwhile, celebrate. Experience the moment together with soft drinks, a cake, cookies, or even a full meal. Watch the alcohol consumption, it could turn a celebration into an event-not-to-be-remembered. Ban alcohol in celebrations on company time.

Birthdays, anniversaries of employment, retirements, transfers, and other noteworthy occasions merit at least a getting together as a team. Express congratulations, and perhaps say a few appropriate words of praise. There are many different ways to accomplish your purpose.

I know of a couple of companies that have monthly get-togethers of all their employees. One or two people cover the phones while everyone else gathers to share cake and punch or coffee. One company combines celebration of the month's birthdays and employment anniversaries. The company president takes a few minutes to give a brief report to all assembled about company progress. Cost is low, lost production time is minimal, and the building of morale is noticeable.

Strategy 6.23

Don't tolerate, remove unsuitable people.

Sometimes we have a tendency not to terminate unsuitable employees as soon as we should. This is particularly true if we have developed close relationships with them, and/or if close bonds have been formed with other members of our team.

This is a dangerous practice and should be avoided. When you determine that an employee is unsuitable to continue as a member of your team, take steps to terminate your employment relationship with that person.

In some cases, your work will have begun already through the progressive discipline process. In other cases, you will have to confront the situation differently. Beware of capriciously terminating any employee abruptly without just cause. Based on your personnel policy manual, which you should create if you don't have one, just cause might include use of drugs or alcohol on company premises, theft, life-threatening behavior, and insubordination.

In either case, you might want to counsel the employee regarding the employee's suitability for continued employment with your organization. Perhaps this person just doesn't fit in. You're probably better off if the employee decides to leave you and resigns.

If the employee does not take the initiate to resign, take the necessary steps to move toward termination. If you allow an unproductive, or counterproductive, employee to remain on your payroll, other employees can become "poisoned" by that person's behavior. It's something akin to the bad apple in the bushel.

Dedicated employees lose faith and respect for you if you do not take decisive action when one of your employees doesn't pull his or her own weight. The good employees become disillusioned, wondering why they're working so hard. Good people want to be surrounded by other good people and have low tolerance for substandard co-workers.

Strategy 6.24
Conduct exit interviews.

Some of your employees will leave your organization just because it's time to move on. Most will leave because of something that happened, or didn't happen. Regardless of the reason, you should know why each of your employees leaves you.

To discover this information, conduct an exit interview with each person who leaves you. Find out what they liked, and what they didn't like, about working for your company. What would they have liked to see different? Why?

Ask about their plans for the future. Where are they going to work next? Why? What does the new employment offer them? How does it differ from what the employee is offered at your company? Would they have liked to remain with your organization; what would have motivated them to stay? What suggestions do they have for making improvements in your company? Would they be interested in returning some day?

Your entire focus during this open, non-threatening interview should be to determine what is happening in your organization that could have caused the employee to look for greener pastures. How can you do things better? Ferret out the problem areas so you can deal with them. Gain a deeper understanding of your organization's strengths so you can use that information in your recruiting.

You can actually conduct sessions similar to exit interviews with your current employees. Find out what they like about working for you. Why do they stay? What improvements would they like to see, and why?

Listen carefully to what people say. Take notes, during the interview or afterwards, to document what you are learning. Meet with your colleagues to analyze what you have discovered and judge the potential impact on other valued employees. Do you need to take any immediate steps to keep others from leaving?

Those managers who do not learn from departing employees why they are moving on, leave themselves wide open for a mass exodus. Stay in touch with the trends in your organization and in your industry.

Strategy 6.25
Establish clear policies.

The people who work with you need to understand very clearly what it is you want from them. They need to understand exactly what your company policies are, why those policies were established, and how tightly they will be enforced.

Company policies cover a wide range of topics, from security of company property to work release for jury duty. There are a number of books and guides available in your library, from local book stores, and from catalog services to help you construct a set of policies appropriate to your organization.

The key, from this book's perspective, is to establish clear policies to govern how things are done in your organization. If you are unable to be clear and definitive, it may be better not to have a policy in a particular area. Unclear policies often create more difficulties than the absence of any policy covering a topic.

To develop policies that best suit your needs, look at the kinds of questions a new employee may have. People who have been with your organization for quite a while will have a fairly consistent understanding of what should be done. They would usually decide each matter the same way. Those established practices can be put down on paper, in most cases, as accepted policies. You may find that a set of policies will be relatively easy to construct by following this process.

There will be other issues where the decision is not as clear-cut. In these situations, senior management must determine what the policy will be and put that statement on paper. Some of the long-term employees may be able to offer some valuable input, based on the way things have been done-- or specifically not done in the past.

Gradually, you can create your own unique set of policies for all to see, understand, and apply. When making them official, be sure to explain the reasons for the policy as well as what each policy is. Understanding the reasoning behind the policies will help employees decide what to do in cases where no written policy exists.

Strategy 6.26
Administer policies uniformly.

Once you have established the policies, exceptions to the rule should be rare. The policies should apply uniformly to all employees and in all situations. If exceptions are justified, say with the way a particular long-term customer is treated, all concerned should be told about that exception.

If there are too many exceptions, your policy is written too tightly. Some fine-tuning might be necessary.

If you are administering personnel policies, they should apply the same way to all members of your team. If you are administering customer service policies, all customers should be treated the same way according to those standards. The same criteria apply to interactions with suppliers and anyone else who deals with the organization.

The standardization provides some of the stability that is so essential to solid, long-term operation of any organization. (*See Strategy 6.8 for a further discussion of the importance of stability.*)

Strategy 6.27
Provide advancement opportunities; promote from within.

When your organization has a policy of promoting from within, your good people will set their sights more deliberately on opportunities for professional growth in your employ. If there are few potential openings and you seem to hire more people from the outside for middle- and senior-management positions, your people will "see the handwriting on the wall," whether it is really there or not.

Good people will look for growth opportunities, for paths to greater career enhancement. If they perceive that those avenues are not open to them with your organization, they will quite naturally look elsewhere.

To hold good people, let them see they have at least an equal chance in the competition against outsiders for high positions. Give credit in comparing applicants to the value of the years of service by your employee. Not only does that individual know something more about the job, but has a deeper understanding of the organization, the personalities in various key positions, and what will be expected of the successful candidate in the new position.

Whenever an outsider is chosen over a home-grown candidate, ask yourself very seriously why you did not choose your current employee. You owe that examination to yourself and to your employee, and you should share the results of your study with the employee. Why was the employee not prepared for the opportunity? Will that same circumstance exist when the next opening occurs? What are you doing to prepare your people to move up in your organization?

If you haven't already done so, it might be wise to invest some time and thought to developing a succession plan. How will people move up in the organization if (name the position) is vacated through promotion, retirement, death, or resignation? (*See Chapter 10, for ideas on preparing people to move up the ladder.*)

A word of caution and concern is in order here. While it is important to promote from within to build stability, longevity, and a strong sense of opportunity, remain open to considering candidates from outside. If all your people in management are from "the ranks," you may limit the infusion of new ideas and perspectives from those with leadership or specialized experience in other organizations. Strive for a balance that demonstrates how you value your people, but select the best candidate for each position.

Strategy 6.28

Give permission to fail or succeed.

It's easy to give your people permission to succeed. Everyone wants to do well and wants others to do well. Our problem comes with the flip side of this coin.

Some of the things people try, particularly if they are innovative and relatively prone to risk-taking, won't work. They may not work as well as expected, or they may just plain flop. Bomb. Fail. Crash and burn.

Don't punish your valued employee for trying. Failures help breed successes. Accept the loss and keep moving. Try something else...quickly. Don't let the hurt fester very long before getting that person involved in another project. The employee will feel badly enough already. You don't have to do or say anything to be sure the employee knows the effort was a failure.

The shame, frustration, and embarrassment are already having a negative impact. Rescue your Don Quixote quickly, dust off the knight and shine up the armor. Emphasize the positive aspects of the unsuccessful effort and move the valued employee ahead in a positive, we-learned-something manner. What can we learn from the next endeavor?

While you don't want to encourage failure, you do want to encourage experimentation, innovation, and the drive to make positive changes. Let people know that you accept the fact that some projects won't do everything we'd like them to. But, that failure brings us that much closer to a success.

Give people credit and support for just trying. Most employees are even afraid to try. Cheer on your risk-takers! They're the ones who can help you make a difference!

If you criticize or punish those responsible for a failure, expect two consequences: first, they'll be reluctant to try something else new while working for you. Second, they'll begin searching for another company that will accept their failures and encourage them to keep trying.

Strategy 6.29

Management Commitment: People are our most important resource.

Every organization uses a number of resources to accomplish its mission. Capital, space, time, equipment, materials, people, and other resources are allocated according to their availability and need.

While all the resources are important, the most valuable is the human resource: your people. Personnel costs are most often the largest portion of the organization's budget. Good people are the most difficult resource to acquire, develop, utilize, maintain, and retain. We can sometimes "make do" with less quality or quantity in another resource, but we need to earn the greatest possible return on our investment in human resources.

Let your people know that they are your greatest asset. Tell them how important they are to the organization's success, and that you appreciate what they do to help achieve success.

People are also your most responsive resource. Through their efforts, people can overcome the weaknesses in other resources. The other resources can't do that to compensate for a weak human resource.

If your building were to catch fire, your first concern would be the safety of the people. Equipment, raw materials, even records, would be secondary. People are your most important resource.

While it would seem to go without saying, it is worthwhile for management to verify through written expression that people are important. Give the support to people, and the rest of the puzzle somehow comes together.

Strategy 6.30
Share information.

People want and need information to make decisions and to get things done. Establish a clear company policy to make every effort to provide the information people need.

Unless you deliberately open the flow and exchange of information, people will tend not to share what they know with others. This tendency is not a malicious withholding of knowledge as much as it is a lack of emphasis on opening up. It's a problem of omission, rather than control or protectionism. We just don't do it unless there is some impetus.

To facilitate the open exchange of information, establish a means of making knowledge available. Reports, summaries of activities, notices on bulletin boards, staff meetings, and teamwork can help get the word out. The opportunity to access information through local area networking of personal computers helps a number of companies.

Sometimes information is not communicated from one person to another, from one department to another, because people are not sure what questions to ask to gain the knowledge needed. This obstacle can be overcome, to a degree, by helping everyone see the "big picture." Once people start relating the parts together, the questions to enhance understanding come easier.

Communications deficiencies are one of the biggest problems that organizations face today. The best way to overcome the problem, even though it's time-consuming, is to schedule meetings where key players can explain to each other what they are doing. The real understanding will come during the question and answer period.

Emphasize to everyone the importance of investing the time and energy to be sure people know what each other is doing.

Strategy 6.31
Value all your people.

Each and every member of your team plays an important part in the success of your organization. They have different roles and make different kinds of contributions, but they all do something to help the overall team achieve its objectives.

Value all of your people. The custodian and the brand-new employee are valuable human beings, valuable team members. In that regard, they have the same kind of value as the president of the company or a long-term employee.

Show your people how much you value them by the way you treat them, the way you care for them. You are probably respected for your position and for your knowledge about the company, the industry, the market. Remember the old adage: "People don't care how much you know until they know how much you care."

Demonstrate your caring for your people. Let them see how much you value them as members of your team. Tell them what is going on. Ask for their advice. Express your appreciation for their efforts in helping the team get its job done.

Strategy 6.32
Respond to complaints with solutions.

When things don't go just right, people usually respond emotionally. Their first step is to gripe. We gripe about everything from the frustration of rush hour traffic to irritation with recalcitrant photocopy machines.

Most of the time, griping is just a way of letting off a little steam. When gnawing problems are not solved, the gripes can escalate into complaints. If complaints are not dealt with properly, they can become grievances and seriously affect performance of the people and the organization.

The answer is to be sensitive to the gripes, but highly attentive to complaints. When one of your people complains about something, respond quickly with interest and concern. Let them know you care about the problem.

Ask for their ideas on how the problem can be solved. Listen to that input, then determine what temporary or permanent solution you can apply. Take action to follow through to assure that the solution is implemented to defuse the complaint and solve the problem.

Unsolved problems that generate complaints become proportionately more serious as time passes. If you don't respond to complaints with viable solutions, people begin to think you don't care. If not managed properly, these attitudes can grow to create a rift between you and your people.

Those who don't want to be part of an organization where there is dissension will be receptive to alternative employment opportunities. Perhaps it's hard for you to envision an unanswered complaint ballooning into a full-blown conflict between leaders and team members, but it happens. It happens more often than we'd like to believe.

Listen for complaints. Listen to what people have to say. Respond with action, not patronizing lip service or promises. Do something.

Strategy 6.33
Use your business plan.

"Plan your work, then work your plan."

That familiar saying rings true again and again. It applies to your efforts to keep your good people.

Employees like to know their management team has some sort of a plan that is used to move the organization forward. More and more, people are interested in the content of the plan, as well as its existence.

An increasing number of companies have established plans that chart the course for all functions of the organization. The role of work teams can be seen as the plan unfolds. People will respond to the expectations of the plan...if and when they become aware of those expectations.

If you have a viable business plan, you can use it as a motivator, as a set of objectives or targets, as a way to get people more involved with the achievement of desired results.

Explain your organization's plan to your people. Help them understand what you are trying to do (big picture) and how they can help make the plan a reality (their picture). As people appreciate the importance of them doing their part, the plan can become a driving force in total team accomplishment.

Each work team strives to get its part done, and done well. As this happens, teams can feed off each other and collaborate for bigger results than any one team can reach on its own. The plan helps bring all these aspects together, so the pieces of the puzzle fit.

As the understanding of the plan grows, and people see that it works over a long enough period of time, you can involve people from all over the organization to help design future plans. This becomes powerful, as people will support what they help to create.

Your plan becomes like a song sheet for a choir. It's a lot easier to make beautiful music when everyone knows his part as well as an understanding of the whole piece.

Strategy 6.34

Within safety constraints, permit refreshments at work stations.

When people are working, they often like to sip coffee, have a soft drink, or enjoy a glass of water. Some folks like to munch on a candy bar or a carrot stick. This snacking might help keep people alert, make them feel refreshed, or satisfy nutritional cravings.

As long as such refreshments, or their consumption, do not endanger safety, quality, or work flow, it's usually a good idea to give people the freedom to snack.

Why mention something like this, you might wonder. Some companies do not even permit employees to drink a cup of coffee at their work station, whether in a manufacturing or office environment. People must leave their work to sip some coffee or tea. They may not want to leave their work; all they want is a cup of coffee or a soft drink.

If company policy forces people to stop their productive work for some refreshment, think of the message that workers could receive. "Being human and enjoying some refreshment is separate from working. Therefore, being human and enjoying what I do is different than work. The concept of enjoyment is not connected with work." Does that sound far-fetched, or very real?

It is usually more productive to engender feelings that personal goals mesh with organizational goals. A worthwhile positive goal from both personal and organizational perspectives is to get work done. Employees should believe, "Meeting my personal needs, like having some refreshment and going to the bathroom, are part of my work experience, not separate from it. My personal energy is well-invested in accomplishing the work I am expected to do. Everything I do supports my meeting or exceeding productivity and job satisfaction expectations."

Give people the freedom to manage their work time, their break time, and the accomplishment of their assigned tasks.

Strategy 6.35
Offer freedom of choice: break times, dress, vacations.

It's important to have rules to set limits in various areas of how people operate in the work environment. But, if you make the rules too tight, too stringent, those people who feel they are mature enough to manage their own lives will object.

More controls are needed in some work areas, such as those with constantly moving assembly lines. The people who work in those kinds of jobs understand that need and will accept the limitations that go along with that sort of work.

The key is not to make the rules any stricter than they absolutely must be. Give people as much flexibility as you can.

Strategy 6.36
Choose employees carefully the first time.

A wise corporate policy to establish and follow is to strive to select the right people to be new employees...the first time.

Surprisingly, a number of employers hire people they think (or hope) will make it. During the probationary period, it becomes obvious that the new hire won't make it. So, that person is let go, and someone else is hired to "try out." Other employees see this continual flow of new hires and begin to wonder about management wisdom, company stability, and future integrity of the workforce. I've heard hourly workers at some companies suggest that the traditional swinging door designated as the "employees' entrance" be changed to a revolving door.

Take time to consider a number of applicants, conduct sufficient interviews, check references, and look carefully at each potential hire. Use aptitude tests, behavioral profiles, skills tests and work try-outs to screen out those who have little chance of success in the job.

Be wary of hiring people with no potential for advancement in the organization. If you bring in a disproportionate number of such employees, you limit your capacity to manage the succession stream. Be very conscious of the place and the potential of each of the people you invite to join your team.

Invest time and other resources in conducting a thorough orientation program. If done realistically, this process may further reduce the number of possible team members. This conscientious screening will increase the success rate in hiring: more people actually hired will stay with the company over the long run.

Careful selection will produce a better return on investment in training, reduce turnover, minimize extra overhead costs in processing people who don't last, and will enable the company to hire the people who will stay with the company over the long haul.

You owe it to your current employees to select new members of your team cautiously. Both the present and future effectiveness of your organization are at stake.

Physical Strategies

There are a number of physical comforts, or lack of discomforts, that are important to people in their workplace.

Employers who ignore such concerns are doomed to lose their best employees to other organizations sensitive to such needs.

Everyone would like a corner office. Or so we are led to believe by some of the popular myths perpetuated by articles in magazines and books. Actually, while some really do want a corner office with all the trappings, most people just want a suitable work area conducive to their task accomplishment. However, they often also want that work area to reflect their value to the organization.

The physical concerns don't focus entirely on the work area. They even extend to the appearance and location of the place of employment. Keep in mind the feelings of the valued team member, in terms of self-worth and comparison to others. Comparison is a natural tendency. Can your people be proud and hold their head high among their peers--inside and outside their organization?

Strategy 6.37
Locate your company in a suitable environment.

To the extent possible, locate your company in an environment suitable to the kind of work you do and where you do it. Consider your employees in making your decision.

While central cities are quite appropriate for many companies, more and more employers are seeking locations in suburbs and smaller outlying towns. If most of your work is done by computers and high technology communications systems, do you really need to be in the high rent district downtown? Messenger services deliver just as well, or better, to locations outside the downtown area.

People who have to fight their way through rush hour traffic jams on highways and sidewalks are under quite a bit of negative stress before they even reach their work site. The commute has eaten away personal time, and during the day they may (un)consciously worry about the risk and hassle of the trip home. This cuts into their productivity. And few people are excited about paying huge amounts of money to park in downtown parking garages, cutting into their take-home pay.

Official work hours in downtown areas of major cities are often 8:00 a.m. to 4:30 p.m. Some employees arrive closer to 8:30 because of rush hour congestion, then have to leave by 4:10 or 4:15 in order to catch a train to get home by a reasonable hour to meet family obligations. Think of the loss of working time on an annualized basis. It can amount to about three and a half weeks a year.

We know of people working in major cities, facing a two-hour commute in the morning and again in the afternoon. Some of these folks try to manage their schedules to work four long days to save the hassle of the commute on the fifth working day of the week.

So, if you don't need to be downtown, consider locating at least part of your people in more accessible, less stressful locations.

Having said that, I must share the counterpoint. Not everyone wants to move out of the city. I'd recommend, if you're contemplating a location change, that you ask your people for their input.

Recently, a company in Cleveland began planning a major move to a suburban location. The company's employees heard about the plans and indicated their desire to remain in a downtown location. Result: the company expanded its facilities in the central city area and everyone is happy.

If a possible expansion or relocation is in your future, consider employee preferences along with availability of essential services, transportation patterns, supplier proximity, costs, available sites, tax incentives, and other factors.

Strategy 6.38

Encourage people to personalize their work areas.

Give people control over the decoration of their work area. Allow them some privacy and an opportunity for self-expression. Some employers worry about what sorts of limits they should place on how someone decorates his or her work area. Usually, the fears are unfounded. People will respect office decorum. If their work area becomes more comfortable for them, they will be more productive and satisfied with their working environment. This feeling encourages them to remain with your organization where they have some personal freedom.

Outside the office area, this same kind of philosophy can apply to production facilities. For safety reasons, there must be more concern for limitations. But, many work areas would allow for display of family photos and perhaps some flowers.

Some manufacturing companies encourage their production employees to paint their machines in a favorite color. True, it may give the plant the appearance of a circus...but, aren't circuses fun? Work should be a fun place to be. If people can enjoy their work environment, they will enjoy their work and be more productive and loyal. Part of them is linked with part of the company.

The same effect can be gained, in many environments, by encouraging tasteful decoration of lockers. The ideas for self-expression are limited only by your imagination, within the bounds of what can be done in your kind of work areas. Not everyone will take advantage of the opportunity to personalize their workspace, but they'll appreciate having the right to do so.

Strategy 6.39
Eliminate reserved personal parking.

Current thinking suggests that reserved parking spaces are passe. They promote status levels that are based on position, rather than on respect for a person's leadership role. If you are emphasizing teamwork in your organization, separately reserved parking areas suggest that some team members are better than others.

The attitude that some people are better than, or deserve more than, others fosters a sense of alienation. Alone, that irritant may not cause someone to leave your team, but combined with other factors, it could become the proverbial straw that breaks the camel's back.

Strategy 6.40
Provide effective communications systems.

High achievers become increasingly frustrated when they have difficulty communicating with other people as they try to get things done. If your telephone system, walkie-talkies, or other communications systems constantly provide irritating problems for your people, the situation could become counter-productive in more ways than one.

Your people know how they need to communicate. Give them the opportunity to present their ideas about how your systems should be designed. With the expanding capacities made possible by today's technology, you should be able to design and obtain the kind of system that will make sense for your people.

An increasing number of companies are using paging systems, often designing private systems that don't utilize outside commercial switching systems. Signals available include tone only, voice, and silent systems that vibrate to tell the person wearing the pager to follow some predetermined response procedure.

Strategy 6.41
Equip people to be productive.

Give people the tools they need to get their jobs done. Waiting in line to use a photocopy machine can inhibit productivity and build dissatisfaction. Not having the right tool to adjust a machine on a production floor can cost time and people.

One of the problems we see in production facilities today, particularly in job shops, is the time it takes to get tooling prepared to run a job. Set-up takes too long; raw material is not available; supervisors or engineers are confused about what the customer really wants. Result, highly paid craftsmen in high demand in the industry become frustrated and critical of management. Another offer comes along, and they're gone.

Good people want to work. They want to do a good job. Give them what they need to perform at peak performance and they will give you the results you seek. Make their work more difficult, and you may soon be replacing them.

Strategy 6.42
Provide for appropriate child care services.

Provide child care facilities and services for your people. You can do this on-premises, in a company-operated facility nearby, or under contractual arrangements with outside providers.

With the increase in the number of working women and the increase in single-parent families, there is a significant concern today for the children of working parents. The concern is not limited to the women in our workforce. Men are sharing more and more in the responsibilities for child care, particularly when the mother is working a different shift.

Employees have a wide range of needs in the child care area. With small children, the need is for competent, caring people to provide for the kids while the parent(s) work. This goes beyond babysitting today, addressing quality and service issues such as planned learning/growth activities for pre-schoolers. The desire for a healthy environment has taken on a more holistic orientation.

School-age children may go home to an empty house, where as latch-key kids they have to fend for themselves. They may go to a neighbor's home, or to a relative or child care provider in the neighborhood. Making these arrangements can be a major challenge for working parents, especially if a key player (including the child) is ill. Expect last-minute problems to occur.

Seek ways to provide for children of your employees. If your employees live and work in the same community, there will be one set of needs and solutions. If there is a distance factor, another set of needs and possible solutions comes into play.

If you don't want to get into the child care business, with its attendant challenges and liabilities, you might consider some sort of cooperative alternative. Nearby employers sharing your circumstances might welcome an opportunity to coordinate efforts and resources. You might jointly contract with an existing or specially-created child care provider to serve your employees exclusively.

Again, before proceeding, talk with your employees who are concerned about child care issues. Solicit their ideas, discover what approaches would best respond to their needs.

Seek creative solutions. You may be amazed at the wisdom, caring and appreciation you'll see from those working parents.

Strategy 6.43
Maintain comfortable atmospheric conditions.

People like to be physically comfortable when they work. A significant part of this comfort results from control of the temperature, humidity, ventilation, light, color, smell, noise level, and cleanliness.

Sometimes one or more of these factors may be outside your ability to control. A stamping plant, for example, will have noise; that just goes with the territory. In consideration of this, the management of that plant could provide a quiet room where employees could take breaks in a pleasant area with less noise.

The more you can do to provide a good working atmosphere for your people, the more they will appreciate it. This is especially true if you do some innovative things that are ahead of, or different from, what your competitors are doing.

Your employees probably have some ideas on things that could be done, and will enjoy being part of generating, influencing, and implementing "cutting edge" ideas. Solicit their contribution to the shaping of their environment.

Strategy 6.44
Use color constructively in decoration.

Psychologists, artists, and decorating professionals will tell you unequivocally that colors have a measurable impact on productivity, comfort, attitude, and job satisfaction. In designing or redecorating work areas, consult a decorator specializing in work environments and/or do some research on your own.

Colors can affect perception of spaciousness or of temperature. For instance, in areas where workers are exposed to relatively high temperatures, cool colors such as light green or aqua will offset the discomfort psychologically.

Soft greens, golds, and blues are said to support worker concentration where you want to minimize distractions and help people see detail better. Reds, oranges, earth tones, and all the rest of the colors in the spectrum have their place in various kinds of work environments.

Bright or contrasting color is more impelling than neutral hues. It can help bring order out of chaos in the eye's perception of the surroundings. Used strategically, color can help workers distinguish important from unimportant elements. An example is the yellow paint used to call attention to safety hazards or zones in industrial plants.

Color should support the task, not distract from it. While the judicious use of color may inspire workers, too much color or the wrong colors may distract people from their tasks. Color should fit the environment, not stand out. You can improve visibility, help people stay organized, and contribute to mental attitudes by choosing the right colors for the work environment.

Strategy 6.45
Provide a safe, secure environment.

While they will endure unfavorable working environments, good people prefer to have surroundings that support their productivity. The less they have to worry about, in terms of their physical environment, the more they can devote their attention and energy to meaningful work.

Your location will influence the safety and security of your facilities. Some locations require more safeguards (and more expense) to secure. Consider socio-economic and other conditions surrounding your work site(s), present and future. Remember that the degree of safety is gauged by statistical reality coupled with employees' perceptions.

Begin your analysis of facility security with the property around your building. Is there a safe parking area for employee use? Are fences, security personnel, video surveillance, lighting systems, or other measures employed to minimize risk to your people?

Next, consider access to your building itself. Are entries as secure as they need to be? Many companies use door controls with security systems, mechanical, electric, or electronic to monitor and control who enters. Some organizations use security guards, armed in some places, to assure protection of people, equipment, materials, and documents.

Some companies provide internal security within the physical structure of a building. An example is restricted access to certain work or storage areas. Even locked file cabinets are part of an internal security system.

Provide special secured areas as needed to protect company and personal property. As an example, a female employee may need to leave her purse somewhere while she moves around getting her job done. The employer should provide locking desks, lockers, or other places where personal belongings may be stored.

Consider your security status when people are working and when they are not working. Can an employee leave papers or project materials out overnight without worrying about their security?

I'm not suggesting that you create an armed fortress, but do consider both your actual conditions and the feelings your people have about their own security while working for you.

Chapter 7

Relationship Strategies

In this chapter, we will consider strategies that revolve around the way we treat the people on our team...and around the ways they treat each other. Positive relationships are essential for retention and productivity. Part of your responsibility is to be attentive to people's personal needs--individually and collectively.

Strategy 7.1
Understand Behavioral Styles.

Understand the behavioral style of each of your team members. The best way to gain this knowledge is through the use of a self-assessment instrument that enables you, and your team member, to understand each other's styles. There are a number of such learning tools on the market today, but we have found the Performax Personal Profile to be the most effective.

A person's behavioral styles, learned throughout life or learned specifically on-the-job, are strong determinants to how that person will function, respond to various motivators, and fit in with the rest of your team.

Some people will be in conflict with each other, quite expectedly, as a consequence of their behavioral styles. Others will be highly compatible and will work extremely well together. Obviously, this kind of information is important to understand and appreciate when you are building a team.

See Appendix A for further information about the four basic behavioral styles and how you can learn more about them.

Strategy 7.2
Understand values and ethical standards.

Be sensitive to people's values and ethical standards. Each of your people grew up learning a certain set of values. If those values are in serious conflict with the values of others in your organization, the person who is different will probably leave to seek a more congruent working environment.

While some discussion may be in order regarding a person's values, you should not attempt to change the person's perspectives. Your role should be to facilitate an understanding of the values, by both the individual and other team members...including yourself.

Discuss also how the team member's values compare to the values of the organization. When faced with irreconcilable differences, it's usually best to part company. Regardless of how talented that person might be, the continuing conflict could be disruptive to the entire group.

Further disucssion on values issues is found in Chapter 6. Appendix B, Personal and Corporate Values, offers additional insight.

Strategy 7.3
Resolve conflicts.

Conflicts will always be present. If they are not dealt with, promptly and constructively, they could easily cost you dearly in time, productivity, future cooperation, or valued employees. They can not be ignored.

If an unresolved conflict goes deep enough, it could destroy a company, particularly as other employees take sides and turn a relatively minor disagreement into an uncontrollable brouhaha. Be alert to potential difficulties among your people. Act promptly in response to developing conflicts before the problems become serious.

Conflicts may deal with work issues, with personality clashes, or outside influences. Conflict is not, in itself, bad. It is often a positive interaction. The key is how the conflict is handled, both by the participants and by you as their leader. Don't hide the conflict, or your involvement in getting it resolved. Get it out in the open so everyone concerned knows that you are aware of the problem and responding to it.

Your role in conflict resolution should be to reduce the emotional involvement that usually accompanies conflict. Help those involved concentrate on the issues that are causing the conflict. Sometimes there are real problems that must be addressed; sometimes the differences are petty or even just imagined by one or more of the parties.

When conflicts arise, recognize that you have an intervention role to play. Conflicts rarely go away by themselves. Some companies have a conflict resolution system established where solving such problems becomes a high priority on the agenda of a senior manager. You can even formalize it to the point of holding hearings to let everyone "ventilate".

While these approaches may be appropriate in some cases, most companies have found that informal resolution at the lowest possible level in the organization is best. Teams are like families. They work beautifully together, but have little problems that have to be worked out from time to time. Consider your team to be like your family and help the antagonists resolve their difficulty.

If the conflict gets blown out of proportion, one of your valued people may feel the need to leave to save face. Solve problems quickly to avoid the need for such drastic response.

Strategy 7.4

Hold meetings of your team members.

Hold regular team meetings to provide opportunities for open communication. These gatherings seem to be most often held on a weekly basis, in companies where they are used. Some organizations get people together on a daily basis, several times a week, bi-weekly, or monthly. Do what seems best for you and your people.

A recommended approach is to hold semi-structured meetings. Have a basic agenda--matters that are usually discussed at each meeting. These topics could include information about new products, new customers, new employees, current employees, or other changes in the routine flow of activities.

It's helpful for people to share, briefly, what they are working on. This lets everyone have a sense of the bigger picture and provides an opportunity for specific input from one person to another. When this involves extensive one-to- one communication, the leader should suggest that the participants meet afterwards to discuss details. Respect the time of all involved.

After the semi-formal portion of the meeting, open the session to the sharing of ideas, problems, gripes, or anything else that anyone has to say. In our work with scores of companies, we are amazed at the lack of opportunities for people to just share with each other.

This togetherness takes a little time, but as long as it is work-focused, it can be highly productive. The investment of a relatively brief amount of company time can reap tremendous rewards in terms of people feeling more a part of the team.

Your people are smart. They are close to the action of what your company is trying to do. Many of them have ideas about how things could be done better, but never share them. Why? "No one ever asked." "I didn't think anyone was really interested." "I did say something, but no one listened."

When ideas come up, make some notes and follow through. Let the entire group know about your follow-through, not just the individual who made a suggestion. This open communication will support the individual who spoke up, and send a clear message to everyone else that you want to hear their ideas and will respond. Even if something suggested can't be done, at least explain why in a positive way so your people will feel encouraged to offer more ideas.

Strategy 7.5
Call spontaneous meetings.

When something comes up that everyone should know about, bring your people together to share the news or the concern. Some things should not be put off until the next regular meeting. The spontaneity alone can be positive in many organizations, especially when the normal course of business is to follow an established routine.

Spontaneous meetings can share good news, problems that need solution now, or news that could be easily misinterpreted through the grapevine. Bringing everyone concerned together for a short time for this kind of a meeting also sends a message that you want them to be involved in the important day-to-day happenings of the company.

People want to feel a part of things. The more you help them feel they have a strong awareness, an opportunity for input, and some control over their destiny, the less likely they are to look for opportunities outside your company. When other employers make positions available, your people will be less receptive to those overtures if they feel a real part of what's happening within their current employment.

Incidentally, not all meetings have to be held in the same place. Different messages are conveyed when you hold meetings in a conference room, the Chief Executive's office, the lunchroom, or in the employees' work areas. Consider the best place to hold meetings, relative to the message you want to convey.

Don't limit your meeting sites to company property. Some companies have been highly effective holding meetings off company premises. An all-employee gathering at a local motel meeting room, a restaurant meeting room, or the meeting room of a nearby church can be very effective. Consider serving light refreshments; it builds comfort and gives people something to do while waiting for the meeting to start. It also shows consideration and a certain amount of generosity and commitment by company management.

Strategy 7.6
Facilitate open communication.

Help people understand the best ways to share various kinds of information...or to seek answers to work-related or personal questions they may have. Each company's culture suggests appropriate ways to communicate; become familiar with patterns in your organization, then institute changes as necessary.

Saying you have an open door policy doesn't reduce the intimidation of your office. Telling people they can take their problems to "Personnel" won't work if their supervisor won't let them leave their work stations. Directing people to communicate more won't make it happen.

Talking with business owners and managers, the problem I hear expressed more than any other is the lack of effective communication between employees, between departments, and between company locations. The complexity of this issue could form the basis for an entire book in and of itself.

Interpersonal communications in the corporate environment is complicated, yet simple. Sometimes we erect or support barriers to communication, often without realizing that we are blocking opportunities or motivations for people to share with each other. Many of those blockages are addressed in other sections of this book; the organizational influences on communications are intricate and interwoven. Much of your problem will be resolved as you focus on the concerns described throughout this book.

Facilitate open communication first by practicing it yourself. In personal contacts, memos, meetings, newsletters, letters, and other means of sharing information and feelings, be open, honest, and thorough. If you are closed, protective, or cagey, expect your people to behave the same way. Set the example, then encourage others to follow your lead. It will take some time, but you will see the progress.

Reward success in communications whenever you find it. Remember that people will emulate what they perceive to be appropriate, favor-winning behavior. Recognize with your praise any project or task done well because of strong, productive communication. Call attention to those situations where communication is done well.

To inspire communications, call meetings of key players and ask questions about what's happening. Have participants explain to each other what they are doing. Look for ways people can work together; encourage them to talk openly about those opportunities in group meetings where others observe the cooperation improving.

Ask interrogative questions (using words like who, when, where, why, and how), then focus the people responding to talk directly to others in the group who could benefit from the answer. After a while, you will be able to pull yourself out of the center of conversation, leaving the other participants to communicate directly with each other. You may need to plant seeds with one or two participants to get the process started, but others will join in if you get out of the way.

Many people will let their superiors, or other people they perceive to be leaders, act as "switchboards" to share information. They will tell you something to be conveyed to another. They will ask you to find out about something that someone else has knowledge of. The more you allow yourself to be a switchboard, instead of having those people communicate directly with each other, the more they will rely on you and not interact productively with each other. Unless you need this control over communications for some reason, let go. If you still need information, ask for it.

Strategy 7.7
Stick up for your people.

You certainly expect loyalty from your people. They expect the same from you. Show people you support them, that you'll back them up.

In the natural course of work, people have disagreements or difficulties of one kind or another with members of other work groups, other managers, or even other companies. When these situations arise, be there for your people. Empower your people to defend their position or to pursue a sought-after solution knowing that you support their efforts.

To be most effective in supporting your people, you need to know what they are doing. "Blind loyalty" is foolish; high awareness is wise. Encourage people to keep you informed about their work and any difficulties they anticipate. Work with them to assure the appropriateness of what they are doing, strengthening their position and efforts. Be able to defend them in a disagreement because you know what is happening.

Obviously, it is much easier to support someone when that person's position is right. When someone is wrong, or if their position is not the best solution or approach, you must be diplomatic and tactful in the way you intervene.

Advice given to parents is to tell an erring child that you love the child, but you're not pleased with the specific behavior you see. The same approach can be applied with an employee who does something inappropriate or who takes an untenable position.

If, as a corporate manager, you can not support your employee's position, be sure you at least support the employee. People know when they are wrong, but still expect you to be there for them.

Take time to learn more about what your employees are doing and help them understand what is right and what is wrong. Or better phrased, explain what is easy for you to

support; explain what would make you uncomfortable, unable
to give them the full back-up they would want.

Be realistic. Remember that while you represent the
employee, you also represent the company. You have to
balance your loyalty on a fulcrum of reasonableness. For
example, an employee may want and deserve a salary increase.
You'd like to see the employee receive greater compensation
for work done, but you are also sensitive to the structure of the
wage and salary program and budgetary constraints. You may
be wise to document your support and your faith in your
employee, but not recommend the increase.

There may be times when you take some big risks taking
an employee's side. Do it when necessary for the good of all
concerned. When you take a risk position, or when you find
you can not provide full support for someone, explain your
position so you are not viewed as unconcerned and
unsupportive.

Remember that people don't expect to get everything they
ask for. But when they don't get something they request or
anticipate, they should be given a full explanation of why you
are responding differently than desired.

Strategy 7.8
Give recognition strategically and deliberately.

When people do a good job, they deserve recognition for
their accomplishment. One popular management philosophy
encourages leaders to "catch people doing something right"
and praise them.

The idea here is to be deliberate, intentional, in your
recognition of the work done by others. Don't wait until a job
is completed, or until the annual performance review. Praise
and appreciation should be shared regularly, and
spontaneously, whenever opportunities arise.

Sometimes recognition is given quietly on a personal basis. Even just eye contact and a smile, or a pat on the back or a thumbs-up gesture are all that's needed. A few words of thanks or a short note are sincerely appreciated by good people who are diligently working to get things done. A little bit can go a long way.

In other situations, the recognition becomes much more significant if you shout from the rooftops, proclaiming your employee's achievement. Well, that may be a little dramatic, but you get the idea. There are times when the praise will be much more appreciated if shared with others. Public recognition can have a very positive impact--on those being saluted, on others who care about them, and on those who could earn the same treatment.

There are numerous alternative means to communicate your messages of satisfaction, appreciation, or pride. These range from the one-on-one expressions to press releases sent to trade or professional publications. In between, you can use letters of commendation (copies to personnel files and perhaps to the employee's home), articles in company newsletters or magazines, plaques and certificates, special parking places for employees of the month, cash awards, dinner for two (and/or with the boss) or a nice evening out, time off, special assignments, flowers, or even a candy bar. The list can go on and on. Be creative! Something unique will make the reward that much more meaningful.

The way you express your appreciation is really a strategic decision. What are you trying to accomplish with the recognition? If your objective is to quietly build an employee's confidence, a personal communication is probably your best approach. If your objective is to strengthen the employee's reputation and stature in the work group, a more public announcement might be appropriate. If your objective is to inspire others or to show off the talent or accomplishment in your industry, a different tactic may be applied.

With an understanding of why you are giving recognition, you can determine the techniques to use. If you have several different objectives, you may well employ more than one technique to communicate your messages to the target audiences. Know what you want to accomplish, design the strategy to achieve your goals, then implement it deliberately.

Giving awards for length of service is appropriate to reward longevity and dedication. However, if people are rewarded only for years of employment, the emphasis is on survival in the system instead of ongoing achievement. Pay attention to the "messages" that people receive as a result of your rewards. Remember that rewards reinforce behavior. What behavior do you want to inspire?

Strategy 7.9
Recognize the "new woman."

A new style of female employee is becoming more visible in the work environment. No longer are women limited to clerical, production, or similar routine tasks. Many women are moving competently and confidently into important management positions. This new generation of women in the workforce is different from their predecessors. This difference opens powerful opportunities and, at the same time, puts many men (and some women) in an awkward position. Traditionalists often aren't sure just how to deal with these "new women".

Unlike the previous generation, today's working women tend to be fiercely independent, risk-taking, pioneering, and tough. These are not traits normally associated with the romantic or social side of women. They demand and deserve equal opportunities for participation, professional growth, advancement, and opportunities to take a significant role when merited and appropriate.

Company owners and managers would be well-advised to open their organizations to this new breed of working woman. You will find that these employees are often assertive, and even aggressive when they feel the situation warrants such a response. They stand up for what they believe and can make a tremendous contribution.

These valuable employees are typically well-educated and, on the average, score higher in IQ tests than their male counterparts. They are characterized as being competitive, smart, politically aware and active on social issues. While they may not instantly understand your "old boy" network, they understand power and politics. They can play the games as well, or perhaps better than their male peers.

A shortage of eligible men and a drive to succeed on their own merits has caused many women to be strongly career-oriented. Your valuable female team members will probably resent suggestions that their place is in the home. The more traditional roles of wife and mother have become secondary for many; in many circles, they are not seen as crowning achievements. Single parenting is on the increase, as are changes in the male's role in the home.

Career women want to retain their identity as women, but at the same time compete equally with men in the working world. This creates internal conflicts between "traditional femininity" and the demand for respect as equals. Be sensitive to the personal career concerns that may be held by your high-performing female employees. They are on the cutting edge of a changing corporate culture and their position is not always a comfortable one. Help them identify and resolve personal or work group issues, but don't try to "take care of everything" for them.

Men are confused about interacting with women on a professional level. The new cultures and interpersonal ethics at work, have little resemblance to chivalry and other old-fashioned values of courtesy and consideration that most men were raised with. No longer is it "ladies first." Women want respect, but in different ways.

Managers, both male and female, should spend time with all their employees to learn about their feelings regarding woman's role in the workplace. While I don't want to make too big an issue of this, it is important. It's one of the changes in our society that can cause sufficient discomfort to motivate good employees, both male and female, to leave insensitive or difficult situations to go to an environment perceived as having less stress.

Our research suggests women want both the rewards and burdens of equality in pay, status, opportunity, professional growth, respect, and influence. Common courtesies, such as opening doors for others, should extend to colleagues of both sexes. Women ask men to forget sexual distinctions. Don't shy away from being critical with women if criticism is called for. Tell it the way it is; don't "be nice" to a woman when you would not behave the same way with a male employee in the same position.

Given our changing demographics, the open nature of our educational system, and the increasing need for good people, we can expect more and more highly talented women to move into vital positions in organizations. To attract the best people, and keep them, take whatever steps are necessary to create and maintain a receptive and supportive work environment.

Strategy 7.10
Recognize other "special employees."

Your work force probably has, or will have before long, employees from a variety of other special backgrounds. How well do you relate with employees such as black people, young people, older workers, mothers returning to work, and others who may not "fit the mold" of your so-called typical employee?

There's a lot of potential for significant contributions from these people, as well as from "non-traditional" employees with longer hair, unusual clothes, or different vocabulary.

Be careful not to let someone's uniqueness get in your way of appreciating their value to your and your organization. Sometimes the people who are "different" can be your greatest asset. In some fields, like the media, research, and other creative endeavors, a personal expression of freedom of thought and behavior is prized.

Re-read section 7.9 with these people in mind. You will discover that much of that section applies to other people as well as your rising female stars.

Today's changing workforce includes a growing proportion of workers with physical disabilities. More slow learners are being trained to function quite well in industrial environments. Wise employers give these employees a chance and usually find that they've discovered a whole new field of dependable performers.

Strategy 7.11
Be patient.

Many people in management positions, and even more frequently in ownership positions, are driven by a sense of urgency. There is always so much to do, and such a high awareness of the pressures to get things done efficiently, effectively, and quickly. And, of course, if an approach or system isn't working, change it. Change can almost become a way of life.

Some of the people working with you can easily adjust and respond to urgencies and changes. Even more can not do what we'd like so quickly and comfortably. This does not lower their value to the organization; quite the contrary in many cases. How happy would you be with someone who rushed through your financial statement just to get the job done in a hurry? Would you want your surgeon to operate against the clock?

Be patient with those who take a little longer than you would to learn something or to accomplish some task or project. Help them understand the big picture, why you are impatient. (Your attitude will probably be obvious, even if you try to hide your impatience.)

If you desire a behavior different from what you perceive, talk with the employee about your concern. Explain your impatience; help others view things from your perspective. Recognize that you won't always be right. People won't always do things your way. You may not want them to. If people can do things their way, and get the job done within the limits you have to work with, give them that freedom.

Look for ways you might be able to help people work more quickly or efficiently. Observe, ask questions, and be open to suggestions about how various tasks might be done better.

Don't expect overnight miracles. People take time to grow. If they're doing mental work, the creative inspiration might not come as quickly as you--or they--would like.

Some people will pace their work efforts to fill the time available. In these cases, it may be wise to have more assignments ready for the employee to work on as soon as the current project is completed. They may produce faster if they know more work is waiting for them. Good people need plenty of work to do. I know good people actively looking for new jobs because they don't have enough to do where they are.

Your good people will want to be productive, to make a difference, so give them that opportunity.

Strategy 7.12
Show respect for others.

Each of the people working with you is an individual. Every one of those people has unique qualities, background, expertise, capabilities, potential, and feelings. Each person's values, ethics, behavioral style, talents, and achievements becomes an important and integral part of the fabric of your team, your organizational strength.

Respect and appreciate what power and potential these people bring to you. Empower them to use their strengths in the most productive and satisfying ways possible. Appreciate that, along with their strengths, they have areas of deficiency. As much as possible, design their jobs so they can contribute on the basis of their strengths, without letting their deficiencies get in their way.

Value the uniqueness of each of your individual team members. Blend their special qualities together with those of others on your team. Emphasize what each of them contributes to the strength of your whole group as an entity unto itself.

Respect the privacy desired by most people in the work place. Allow them a place where they can find some solitude or at least call their own. People like to have a special place where they can put things they own or use. Enable them to have their own "space."

High achievers need freedom to do their thing. Respect the fact that many of your people might need to prove something on their own before introducing it to the rest of their work group. Give them the place, the time, and the resources to do what they believe is important.

Naturally, they should have an accountability to perform for the good of the group, and most will do so most of the time. If it is appropriate, articulate your expectations and your support. High performers need to understand what others want, what they have to offer, and what support they have to get their job done.

Some highly valued people are not as polished or sensitive in their interpersonal skills as they are in their own particular talent. You may need to invest some time and energy in helping others appreciate what these folks have to offer. Build those bridges of understanding, from both directions, and you will increase the return from all concerned.

Building relationships in the work place is a vital responsibility of leaders. You will naturally be concerned with professional relationships more than social, but you should play a stimulating, connecting role in helping people appreciate each other.

Strategy 7.13
Give people freedom and flexibility.

The adults who work for you want to be treated like adults. They want freedom to make some decisions on their own, to be in reasonable control of their own lives. They enjoy freedoms outside the work environment and don't want to be constrained when they come to work.

Find ways to give your people freedoms and choices. Some are very simple; others are more complicated in their implementation. Let's look at some possibilities.

Other than in the uniformed careers, people should be entitled to choose the clothes they wear to work. Before you say, "of course", please know that there are employers who still require their employees to wear white shirts in office environments. The men are not allowed to wear any colors or designs in their shirts. Some companies require women to wear skirts; slacks or pant-suits are not permitted. Such restrictions may stifle creativity and productivity. Within the limits of workplace decorum, give your employees as much flexibility as you can. People understand limitations based on safety or propriety, but not arbitrary rules.

More than we've seen in the past couple of generations, today's workers are sensitive to their relationships outside work. With both parents working in an increasing number of families, employees work consciously at maintaining healthy family life. They like to have pictures of their families at their workplace to serve as happy reminders and as a way of showing their pride in their children and grandchildren.

It's important to give people the freedom to display pictures of family and similar personal items. Office workers can put pictures on their desks or walls. Factory employees can attach pictures to their lockers or put them near their work station.

The creativity continues for all kinds of employees...if you give them the opportunity. It's hard to believe, but there are still employers today who refuse to allow their valued people the freedom to display a spouse's photo on their desk. For other ideas that relate to this strategy, see chapter 6, Environmental Strategies.

How much freedom can you give employees to set their own working hours? While some jobs simply don't have the flexibility to allow modification of the work schedule, many do lend themselves to flex-time, job-share, or other approaches to adjustment of start and finish times. There are a number of reasons employees want more control over their schedules (*see Strategy 6.19, Provide flexibility in working hours*). Strive to accommodate them.

Looking at the work itself, some of your people may be able to modify the way a job is done. They may have suggestions about procedures that, while not consistent with existing company policy, might make a lot of sense. Be alert to opportunities, and flexible enough to be responsive to ideas your people have. Ask for input...and listen to what your employees contribute when they believe they really have the power to make positive changes.

When people fully understand the results they are expected to accomplish, you can give them freedom to determine for themselves how they will achieve those results. Workers can often vary the order in which they do things, vary the sequence of jobs they perform, or pace themselves differently to work more comfortably or efficiently and still achieve the results.

Can your people schedule their vacations to fit the needs and desires of their families? Can they work *directly* with their counterparts in other departments to solve problems or get things done? Can they take breaks on their schedule, rather than only at times specified by the company?

Given sufficient information, most people can make the right decisions among the choices available. The more power they have to distinguish for themselves among those choices, the more responsible and happy they will be.

Strategy 7.14
Trust your people.

If you can't trust someone who is a member of your team, that person should not be working with you.

The first question to ask is, very simply, why don't you trust your employee? Has something been done by that employee that causes you not to trust? Is it something you are directly familiar with, or is your evidence hearsay? If your knowledge is not direct and personal, you owe it to yourself and your employee to verify the facts.

If the employee did, in fact, do something to effect your level of trust, was that action a one-time occurrence or is it a continual problem? If it was a one-time thing, are you holding an unfair and unwarranted grudge? Harboring such feelings could inhibit your effectiveness as an inspiring leader and could be severely limiting for your employee's career.

If the problem shaking your trust was continual, has the problem stopped? If it has stopped, can you put the matter behind you? How can the employee restore your trust? If it has not stopped, then you need to confront the employee, express your concerns and your feelings, and bring the matter to some sort of closure. That resolution will either be termination of employment, transfer to someone's else's area, or clearing up the misunderstanding and re-establishing the trusting relationship.

When you do trust your people, do they know it?

There are two ways to verify your trust so your people will produce more comfortably and confidently for you. One method is to express your trust matter-of-factly in words that are easy for you to say. There's no need to get flowery about it. Just tell the trusted employee how you feel. Yes, this will be difficult for some people...especially those who have trouble or discomfort sharing their feelings. Do it anyway; the feeling you will experience afterwards will be worth it.

The other way to demonstrate your trust in an employee is to give the employee a position or task where your trust is an obvious prerequisite. Those who receive important assignments given only to trustworthy team members feel pretty good about the "givens" that are usually left unsaid.

When you share privileged information with someone else, that also shows your trust. Depending on the nature of the information, and your reason for sharing, you may also send the employee clear signals that you value that person's opinions and/or judgment. The words, "this is confidential", also convey your high level of trust.

Yes, it is good to trust your people. It is even better to trust them and have them know that you trust them.

Strategy 7.15

Show genuine, sincere appreciation.

Using "genuine" and "sincere" together almost sounds like a redundancy, but it isn't. The appreciation you show to your people must be genuine; it must be real. And it must be sincerely shown; people see right through insincerity.

Give appreciation when it is deserved. Find legitimate reasons to compliment or thank people. Most of the time, actions, performance, or results worthy of appreciation will be obvious. In other cases, you may have to look a while.

There are things deserving of attention and praise that are not easy to see. Many of your employees will simply do what has to be done without bringing their achievements to your attention. Some may even be modest and make a conscious effort not to bring things to your attention. They don't want to be a nuisance or cause a stir. Some of your most conscientious employees will not want to call attention to themselves. They are proud of their work, but are not comfortable bragging about it.

Reward "final" achievements like completion of a project or special assignment, but also give praise while good things are in progress. Don't just wait till something has been done to tell your people you approve of their work.

Look for the positive aspects of your organization and the good results being achieved by your people. Find out who is responsible for those positives and show your appreciation. It may be that one particular person is worthy of praise, but often you will find *more* than one member of your team who should be recognized. As has been said by more than one management guru, "catch people doing something right."

If you don't see outstanding achievements shouting for recognition, keep looking. You may find some routine accomplishments that deserve your attention. Some managers and advisors warn us not to reward people for doing routine things like coming to work on time or picking up after themselves.

I feel differently about this issue. Many employees do those "part of the job" things every day without anyone ever thanking them. Yes, those things are *expected*, and that's why people get paychecks. However, if we don't thank our employees for the routine tasks once in a while, they will probably feel taken for granted.

Even without significant achievements on any sort of frequent basis, each of our people deserves praise just for being a valued member of our team. Not every day, but every once in a while, it makes sense to thank people for coming to work.

An example of routine work worthy of praise might be helpful to clarify and emphasize this issue. Your bookkeeper, accountant, or controller keeps your financial house in order. Part of the job. Suppose that routine work were not done as well as it hopefully is done. You could be in a real mess! Those people are doing a fine job for you, even though their accomplishments don't usually leap forward for attention. That kind of valuable routine work is deserving of a word of thanks once in a while.

An opportunity awaits you here. Think of all the unsung heroes in your organization. Start making a list of all the fine folks who may not be in the kind of position that normally gets a lot of attention or commendation. Consider all those special people who, by getting their job done well each day, keep your entire system running smoothly. Here are some thoughts: receptionist, custodian, clerk-typist, mail room employee, gardener, security guard, busboy, driver.

Sincerity is critically important. If you are the least bit insincere in your appreciation, it will be apparent to your people. Therefore, a word of caution: if you don't really mean it, don't say it.

Your expressions of appreciation will be much more meaningful if they come from you personally. A letter of commendation, for instance, is much more significant when it is hand-delivered by you instead of through the mail. It takes on even more importance when you convey your appreciation directly to the deserving employee(s) in the presence of peers.

Contrary to some popular opinions in working America, appreciation does *not* have to be in the form of more money in the pay envelope. Sure, everyone wants more money. None of us ever has enough. We can always find things to do with more. Few people will decline a pay increase or cash bonus. While some will surely say they'd rather have money, there are other ways to show appreciation.

Why not just use money? First, it creates an expectation that good work--or even routine work--will be rewarded with more money. A what-have-you-done-for-me-lately attitude will generate ill feelings if people do not receive continual increases in income. Second, by rewarding average or good or exceptional behavior with money, you can easily establish a precedent...and a basis of measurement.

You can get caught in the trap of not knowing how much money to award for each kind of achievement. You can be sure your employees will be monitoring the amounts and placing artificial values on various kinds of rewarded behavior. Be careful. Be clear that each achievement is judged independently, with the reward appropriate for the individual as well as the performance. Avoid precedents.

An exception (isn't there always an exception?) is the program used by a number of companies to encourage and reward suggestions that save money. When employees make suggestions for changes in procedures, suppliers, materials, or other factors that result in a savings, employers pass on a percentage of the documented savings to the person making the suggestion. If you implement such a system, establish specific guidelines regarding calculation of the savings, the amount to be shared with the employee, and the duration of the determination period.

Some other ways to recognize performance or achievement are, in no particular order:
- a word of thanks
- a personal recognition and praise in front of peers
- a quiet, one-on-one word of thanks
- a letter of commendation, with copy to personnel file and perhaps copies sent to the employee's family and posted on a bulletin board or even announced through an employee or community newspaper

- a certificate (framed) or plaque
- a special parking place (employee of the month)
  dinner for employee and spouse with boss and spouse
  tickets to theatre, concert, ball game, or other event
- a special assignment of importance
- a day off with pay
- a pin, certification patch, ball cap, tee shirt, or other
  item of clothing or attachment to clothing
- job title change, promotion, or new position
- priority position in choosing vacation days or working
  hours or other workplace variables
- pizza party, lunch on the company, or dessert treat

And the list goes on. Be creative. Seek unique ways to show your appreciation to the people who make your team success possible.

Depending on your company's culture, you might be quiet and conservative or wildly flamboyant. Ask your team members for their ideas; you'll probably get some wonderful ideas and maybe even some crazy, off-the-wall suggestions that just might be appropriate in some cases. Be receptive! Be responsive.

Remember, your praise is not for your benefit. It's for the benefit of the recipient(s). If they deserve recognition for something, they should get what they deserve. They will half-expect it from you. They'll be overjoyed (at least inside) when you reward them. Don't worry about those people who seem grumpy or unappreciative; remember, some folks just don't know quite how to receive your plaudits. Inside, they probably feel warm and happy that you noticed and you care.

One final word of caution. Don't overdo appreciation. Make it legitimate. Reward and recognize when it is appropriate. If you do it too often, the act loses importance and value. Make it special.

Strategy 7.16
Listen.

Probably the most important communications skill is listening. We learn the most through listening, and other people appreciate us when we really listen to what they have to say.

Interestingly, listening is the one communications skill we don't teach in our formal education system. We teach speaking, writing, and reading, but we don't teach people how to listen effectively. We learn how to listen by ourselves, with varying degrees of success.

Some of our listening strength is a part of our behavioral style (see Appendix A). People with some styles of behavior naturally listen better than people with other styles. Most of us have to work consciously at being good listeners. It doesn't come naturally.

We learn listening skills as adults through trial and error, or simply by trying harder. Participation in listening workshops given by professional trainers has helped countless executives, managers, supervisors, salespeople, and others enhance their ability to listen better.

There are a number of listening techniques we teach in workshops. While we can't devote too much space to this important topic, let's examine a few of the things you can do:

● Block out as many distractions as you can. Closing an office door may remove most of the noise distraction. Having someone take your phone calls can allow you to concentrate without interruptions. Focusing consciously on the person to whom you are listening will help; depending on the nature of the communication, you might need to use intense concentration to hear what is being said.

● Face the person to whom you are listening. This body positioning accomplishes a couple of things for you. First, it communicates plainly that you are giving the talker your full attention. This builds the confidence and comfort of the other person. Second, it enables you to use your senses of both hearing and sight to listen.

- Use your eyes, your ears, and your "sixth sense" as you listen. Pay attention to the words that are spoken, the tone and volume of the person's voice, and the intensity of the communication. Listen for both content and feelings. Go beyond the words to grasp the meaning and intent of the speaker. Sometimes the emotion shown is much more meaningful than the words used to convey a message.

- When appropriate, take notes on what the other person is saying. This technique accomplishes several things for you. It shows the other person you are serious and caring enough to write down their message; this suggests you will probably do something as a result of the communication. It helps you organize what is being said, making more sense of the message as you write it. (Some of us are more visual learners than auditory.) A third benefit of writing key points is having a set of notes to use in responding to the other person in a more prepared fashion.

- Control your own emotions and tendency to respond before the speaker is finished talking to you. Isn't it annoying to have someone start responding to what you're saying before you're finished? The practice is not only rude, but your thinking about what you will say will cause you to listen less effectively to what is being said to you.

Remember that your objective in listening is to gain a clear understanding of what the other person is sharing with you. It is not to defend, argue, direct, inquire, or give people the answers they seek. Your whole purpose is to grasp what is being conveyed. Then, equipped with strong comprehension, you can respond in a way that will best achieve the goals of your conversation. You can't talk and listen at the same time.

We have two ears and one mouth for a reason, it is said. We should listen twice as much as we talk. To learn, close your mouth and open your ears. Ask a few interrogative questions (using open-ended inquiries like who, what, when, why, where, and how) instead of limiting questions that can be answered with a simple yes or no. Keep the other person talking long enough to gain the knowledge and feeling you need to respond legitimately.

Practice a technique known a "active listening" whenever emotions are high, the issue discussed is sensitive, or you are unfamiliar with what is being told to you.

Active listening is a cooperative two-way communications process. It assures both participants that the messages are getting through in a clear, concise, understandable form.

As the term is usually used, active listening employs feedback as a mechanism to assure accurate communications. When someone talks to you, as the listener you paraphrase when you heard and feed that back to the speaker. It's a deliberate, almost formal, kind of interchange.

Listeners begin their response to speakers with phrases like, "if I understand you correctly, you said...," "so, what you're saying is...," "then the essence of your message is...," and "to be sure I understand what you mean...." These phrases are followed by a synopsis or recapitulation, in the listener's words, of what the listener heard.

The speaker, responding to the listener's reaction, then confirms that the communication has been received as intended. If the listener didn't quite get the message, the speaker indicates that there is a problem and endeavors to restate the communication so the listener can better grasp the meaning.

Active listening can be initiated by the speaker as well. After saying something, the speaker can ask the listener for response to make sure legitimate communication occurred. The speaker would say something like, "I'd like to be sure I've explained myself clearly. Would you please share with me what you heard me say?" You'll be more effective with an almost apologetic request, as opposed to a demand.

This process works best when done in a conscious, cooperative way. Confrontation and defensiveness will reduce the effectiveness of the technique considerably.

In the phrases shown above, please notice the use of "I" words in assigning responsibility. The initiator of the active listening process assumes the burden for assuring the accuracy and completeness of the communication.

For best results in applying these, and other listening techniques, remember that listening is serious business. It takes careful concentration, a real desire to hear the other person, and honestly understand what is being said.

Strategy 7.17
Let people be who they are.

Your team of competent people is comprised of a wide variety of interesting folks. Chances are they come from diverse backgrounds, have disparate kinds and levels of formal education, have unique combinations of talent and ability, and are driven by different kinds of motivations.

One of the reasons your team functions well is the individualistic nature of your team members and the special way they complement each other. If your team membership is too homogeneous, you'll have much less opportunity for healthy conflict and creativity.

With homogeneity, the clones will become so like one another that the group's uniqueness will evaporate. Life will become bland due to the overwhelming sameness. Atrophy will set in, kicking the group back to mediocrity and apathy.

Diversity is healthy. Encourage your people to be who they are, not try to be like someone else within the organization. Sure, you might like to operate like the president, but when you play that role you lose some of the value you have in being just like you.

Accept each of your people for who they are. Each will
bring something different to the party. Your opportunity as
team leader, is to mold the diversity into something each of the
members can identify with. At the same time, it is important
that members not lose the uniqueness they have to offer.

Strategy 7.18
Find opportunities to talk with your people.

Interestingly, one of the reasons people leave companies
is because of a lack of a satisfactory relationship with the boss.
While I'm not suggesting that you should establish a close
social relationship with your people (or that you shouldn't), it
is important to develop and maintain some sort of one-to-one
rapport with them.

Today's workers want to know their leader really cares.
They want to see and talk with that leader, have some sort of
personal contact. It is the fulfillment of this need that makes
the Hewlett-Packard Management-By-Walking-Around
(MBWA) technique so effective.

You don't have to invite each of your people into your
office for an in-depth conversation on the meaning of life as
we know it. But you do have to get out of your office and talk
with the members of your team. You have to see and be seen
throughout your organization.

Your closest relationships will be with your direct reports.
These people, of course, need more of your time and input.
They can give you some suggestions regarding other people in
your company that will be most receptive to your
communications overtures.

On a regular basis (not a schedule, please), get out of your
office and wander around your facility. If you are responsible
for more than one physical location, deliberately plan visits just

to be there. Your presence shows you care, that you really do exist, that you are human, and you do look like your pictures.

As you wander, stop and talk with people. Ask how they're doing, or what they're doing. Give production workers, for instance, an opportunity to brag to the Big Boss about how they do their job. Share some things with them about your pride in what they are doing, your appreciation.

You don't have to be the president of a huge conglomerate to be perceived as being in an ivory tower. The same kind of distance can occur in a one-location operation if the leader is not relatively closely involved with what is happening.

If your organization is small enough, you probably should be right out in the middle of things on a constant basis. You have to be the judge of what frequency is most appropriate. Remember, the closer you are to the action, the more chance you have of positively influencing results.

If your schedule is too demanding during the normal working day, try to arrange to greet people as they come to work or go home. Attend company informal functions, such as bowling league nights or celebrations. Company picnics are, of course, a must. When families are there, invest your time with them, too; get to know them and let them get to know you. Employees with families loyal to the employer are less likely to leave that employer. Family influence keeps them where the spouse and kids are included and appreciated.

Merely wandering around and observing is not sufficient. You have to talk with people. Long conversations are not necessary, just enough communication to allow you to demonstrate that you don't think you're better than they are.

Warning: as people become more comfortable with you talking to them, they'll start talking with you. They will ask questions and make suggestions that will keep you on your toes. Be sure to respond with the same speed and attention you would give a customer or other important person.

The people who work with you are the most important people you know in your business life. You can't achieve your desired results without them.

Strategy 7.19
Balance praise and criticism.

As you give feedback to your people, be careful to maintain a balance of praise and criticism. If they think they hear more of one or the other, employees can form impressions that can be counterproductive to what you are trying to achieve.

Praise is good. People like to hear they are doing a good job. They like to know they are appreciated. However, if you give too much praise, it begins to sound empty and loses its impact.

Even with a top-notch employee, it's important to mix some constructive criticism with the praise. If you can't find something with room for improvement, worthy of meaningful critique--which can be done in a positive way, ask the employee. A question addressing how the employee thinks his/her work can be improved will help balance the praise load. Interact with your high-achieving employees in such a way as to let them know you want them to keep growing...and that you are there to help them become even better than they are.

Too much negative criticism can be even more damaging. Some people get so much bad news about their performance, they begin to have negative thoughts about themselves--especially as they relate to their lives working for you.

For people who are vulnerable or sensitive, even a little criticism without a counterbalancing dose of praise will make them feel put down. Some folks very easily feel put down so badly, they have to look up to see their shoes! This does not build positive feelings!

If people feel fairly good about themselves, then experience a lot of negative criticism at work, they quickly associate negative feelings with that work environment. In such cases, those people will take the first reasonable alternative employment opportunity that comes along.

It is not necessary to keep a log of the number of negatives versus the number of positives shared with each employee. Just be alert and sensitive not to go overboard in either direction.

Strategy 7.20
Build everyone's self esteem.

People will naturally perform better when they feel good about themselves. When that good feeling is associated with their relationship with their employer, a stronger bond is felt between employee and employer.

Self esteem should not be confused with self image. The concept of self image refers more to looking good to others, an outward appearance. Self esteem is an inner feeling of personal worth. Self image without self esteem is a role, a façade. Self esteem is the foundation.

To help your people build their self esteem (and each person has to do this internally--we can not do it for them), there are several things you can do. In no particular order, they are:

- create opportunities for personal growth and confidence-building
- reinforce people for who they are
- accept people for themselves
- value everyone's worth highly.

Today's forward-looking thinkers forsee a vital role for self esteem in organizational identity, strength, and success. This attention to personal self-perception takes on increasing

importance as we become more oriented to a workforce of
individuals. Self-esteem is integral for specialists, for those
who play a relatively small part, and for those managing in a
rapidly changing work environment.

*For a further understanding of this concept and critical
importance in organizations, see Appendix C for an exclusive
interview with Bill McGrane, Director of The Self Esteem
Institute.*

Strategy 7.21
Don't gossip.

Gossip and rumors can easily have a negative effect on an
organization. The result can be feelings of discomfort,
suspicion, and even paranoia among members of the
organization.

It's hard to be productive and feel positive about your
position when you are constantly worried about what others
are saying about you. The need to protect yourself from what
you perceive to be personal attacks gets in the way of both
production of good work and personal satisfaction on the job.
When you have to watch your back, it's difficult to look forward
at the same time.

You won't be able to stop all the gossip and rumor-
spreading in your organization. Some people engage in this
kind of activity almost as a hobby, or a diversion from what they
are supposed to be doing. What you can do is set an example
by not engaging in gossip or rumor-spreading yourself.

When you have something to say to or about someone, do
it directly. Don't complain to others about your attitudes when
that won't solve your problems. Confront issues with others
on a one-to-one basis. Even though there is a natural tendency
to talk about others, guard what you say yourself. Be
particularly careful not to spread negative news that may affect

someone's capacity to continue to serve your company comfortably.

When you hear others gossiping, intervene as appropriate and discourage the practice. You don't have to get formal about this. Just quietly suggest to those gossiping that such behavior is not desirable in your organization.

Some high performers rise above the gossip and don't let it bother them at all. Some are highly sensitive to their interpersonal relationships and won't stay in an environment where they think others talk about them in inappropriate ways. Even those who ignore gossip can be affected by it, as co-workers form opinions that affect their working conditions and relationships.

As you create and maintain an open working environment, the closeness and positive feelings among your team members will naturally limit potentially damaging gossip. This issue is not something that requires formal action, as much as a sensitivity to the informal interactions among people.

Strategy 7.22

Look for positives, not negatives.

It's easy to see the negative aspects of practically any situation. Finding things to criticize does not seem to be a problem for most people. Spotting the *positive* things is sometimes more challenging, and perhaps not as much fun.

To overcome natural tendencies, we have to focus on the good things in our lives...and in the lives of our people. Frankly, it is not as simple as it seems. It is something we have to do with a high level of consciousness and intention.

When all you seem to see is the negatives, the shortcomings, your people will categorize you as being more critical than supportive. Before long, they will avoid coming to you or inviting your input. No one likes to hear negatives all the time. As they endeavor to protect themselves from your criticism (nitpicking?), your key people will withdraw and avoid doing anything that might be attacked.

Not saying anything, or doing anything, when positives are there (or thought to be there) to be noticed, can be just as bad--or even worse--than saying negative expressions.

So, the message is: find positive aspects in anything you see. Even when you know the negatives are there, and even if you have to say something about the negatives, be sure to emphasize the positives. Let people save face and feel pride about those things that are good.

A word of warning: Beware of "yes, buts" in your speaking. It can be self-defeating to say something like, "you did a fine job with this, but...." The "but" neutralizes the positive comment, and may even overpower it. In this kind of a situation, many people go around nervously waiting for the other shoe to drop.

Employees can quickly tire of not hearing the positive things they want to hear. Hearing the negatives only wears people down--something they don't want to happen. No one likes living under a dark cloud for very long.

In your communication with others, be realistic. And wherever possible, brighten up your life and your environment with a positive approach.

Strategy 7.23

Express confidence in your people.

Confident employees are more productive employees. They feel better about themselves, about what they are doing, and about their place and value in their working environment. As a result, they have a greater tendency to remain in an employment situation where they feel confident.

Employees get their feelings of confidence from two different sources: external and internal. You, as the leader of your people and a principal influencer of their environment, can have a significant positive impact on both of these important sources.

External sources of confidence include your personal relationship with your team member. You send clear messages, consciously and unconsciously, that express your feelings. When you have confidence in someone, it's wise to express that confidence. Telling people you have faith in them, that you believe in them, that you trust them, that you respect them, or simply that you have confidence in them, will have a great impact. Employees want to know how their superiors regard them, since that affects their present and future career positioning. It also affects how they feel about themselves.

Other external sources of confidence are fellow employees, management people beyond their own supervisor, customers, suppliers, and peers employed by other companiesin the industry.

You can build your employees' confidence in themselves by passing along to your people the thank-you notes and expressions of confidence you receive from customers and suppliers. As appropriate, you might even solicit letters from satisfied customers so you have something more to share with your people.

We could all do a lot more to share feelings of confidence and appreciation within our organizations. Our achievements are often possible only because of the support we receive from others in our company. We take that support for granted, don't we? It's easy to just keep moving in our lives, rarely taking time to express our confidence in those people who make our success possible. When is the last time you sat around the table in a staff meeting and shared your mutual confidence with your peers?

Hearing how your fellow managers, at your level and perhaps a level above and/or below, feel about you could really boost your morale and self-esteem! Hearing others express how much they respect your knowledge, experience, talent, ability to get things done, insight, and leadership would sure make you feel good! Your people get the same "high" hearing that sort of affirmation.

When people appreciate each other and feel closer to others because of those shared feelings, they become more of a team. The more cohesive that team, because of shared attitudes, respect, and experiences, the less likely it is that people will want to leave the team. Moral: if you want to hold your people and help them feel part of a team, encourage them to share their positive perceptions of each other...and of the team itself with the combined strength of the members.

How can this sharing be done in a non-threatening, comfortable way? There are several methods.

The first one is to express your own feelings, setting an example for others to follow. Remember the potential impact of a role model.

A second way is to gather together from time to time those people who work together. It could be a project team, a group of peers from cooperating departments, or managers of facilities in several locations. Create the mix of people in whatever common threads seem appropriate. When people are together, get them talking about possible solutions to a shared problem or a problem they can all relate to.

After they have worked on the problem for a while and have become comfortable interacting with each other, change the subject. Focus their attention on themselves and have participants share what they saw as the positive contributions made by each other. Have them explain why they feel fellow group members can help the group solve the current problem and other problems that challenge the organization.

A third method of sharing confidence and appreciation is to have people write little notes describing their respect and confidence in others. You can do this in a group setting by putting pages of a flip chart on the wall or on tables. Put each person's name at the top of a page and let participants wander around the room writing their comments under each person's name.

Outside the group setting, you can have people write their comments on 3" X 5" cards, putting the name of the described person at the top of the card. You can collect all the cards and distribute them to the described individuals, or you can post them all on a wall or on a bulletin board. This does not have to be a scheduled exercise; create a special place in your facility to post cards or notes...an "I like you because" board.

Customers and suppliers may express their confidence or appreciation for your people. Whenever this happens, be sure the positive messages are posted, circulated, or announced so everyone knows that so-and-so earned some valuable recognition from the outside organization. Notes or letters could be posted on the "I like you because" board for all to see. Be sure a copy goes into the employee's personnel file.

Internal sources of confidence for your people are personal competence and experience. See chapter 10 for strategies to foster growth to build competence among your people. The more people learn, the more they feel they know, the more confident they become about their work.

The same applies to experience. The more experiences a person has, work-related and not, the more confident that person will be. Work experiences, life experiences, and just general exposure to what's going on in the real world, can build confidence. Sending production people, supervisors and hourly workers, to a trade show or a customer visit, can expand horizons and provide new perspectives. That helps build confidence.

Strategy 7.24
Enable people to be together.

Strengthening relationships through social contacts as well as business contacts will build confidence and cooperation. Arranging for people to meet, with or without an agenda, to work on a project together or just talk, can have a positive impact.

There are a number of things you can do, as a leader, to facilitate people getting together, feeling more comfortable together, and functioning better together as a team. Interestingly, we complain a lot about our people not working together, not communicating, but we don't do some of the things we could do to build that togetherness.

You won't usually have to "force" people to come together. Most will welcome your initiation of opportunities for greater communication and interaction. Let's consider some approaches you might take to build relationships.

People eating a meal together can strengthen bonds of friendship and cooperation. Eating together is one of the oldest methods to break down barriers of distrust, ignorance, and fear. Our history books and legends are full of stories of enemies or strangers breaking bread together to resolve their differences or better understand each other.

You can arrange meals on a personal or small group basis. Inviting one or two people to join you for breakfast, lunch, or dinner can set the stage for resolving an interdepartmental conflict, investigating or introducing new policies, building relationships, or just sharing valuable information about the industry or the company. A small group is more intimate and gives you more of a chance to interact personally with each person. It also enables you to give more attention to fostering stronger bonds between those present.

A series of meal-based meetings can encourage partnering between persons A and B, then A and C, then B and C, then

A, B, and C. It may take some time, but gradually you can enhance the way people work with each other.

The larger the group you are bringing together, the more you may want to consider using a more formal agenda. As the number of participants increases, the gathering becomes more of a meeting than a social interaction. To overcome this tendency, design your seating to make communication easier. Having six or eight people at a round table, for instance, will open more communication than having those people sitting across from each other or as part of a larger group at long banquet tables.

Meals can be formal or informal. They can take place in restaurants, in company facilities, or at meeting sites such as hotels, conference centers, or resorts. Many companies design management and sales meetings deliberately to encourage more open communication among participants. It makes it easier for people to share their experiences, ideas, problems, and solutions.

I've seen some companies host quarterly or bi-monthly breakfasts for all their employees. Lots of round or four-person square tables are set-up, so people are eating in ad-hoc small groups. People from all levels and departments of the company enjoy eating and talking together.

In some gatherings, you may want to ask participants to talk together about particular company problems or concerns. This deliberately creates an environment where people with varying backgrounds have been brought together as a company team to accomplish something. This approach can be very powerful, especially if you have already had some meal gatherings where you *didn't* ask for help. Now you come to them, as a team unto themselves, and ask for their input.

There are benefits to all these approaches, depending on what you are trying to accomplish. Consider what you are trying to do, then design the best strategy to meet your goals.

A final word on meals. In our society, people place different values on sharing breakfast, as opposed to lunch, as opposed to dinner. Lunch is most convenient. Dinner is sort of special because it is usually after working hours and more formal. Breakfast is a little inconvenient; it may require an adjustment in schedules.

Breakfast is favored by many leaders because it is at the start of the day, is less formal, and can be concluded more quickly than a lingering dinner. Alcoholic beverages are not a part of breakfast meals, where they may well be a part of lunches or dinners. It is wise to avoid consumption of alcohol in the kind of sessions we're describing, so everyone can operate with a clear head.

Other ways to bring people together include sports activities. These can range from bowling leagues, to softball teams, to company-sponsored participation in charity walkathons. Both organized programs and informal activities can be effective meeting and communications opportunities.

Another way to bring people together is to recruit volunteers from your company to support civic activities such as United Fund, Junior Achievement, Boy Scouts or Girl Scouts, or industry education programs. The additional benefit of doing something, as a company, to support your community will also be worthwhile.

Company picnics are traditional in many organizations, with varying degrees of success. The picnics are more successful if they involve people from all levels of the organization. I am amazed when I learn about managers and senior executives not attending company picnics. Participants get a message from that lack of attendance, regardless of whether that message was intended by management. When management people go to company picnics, they should make a point of circulating among all the people present to become better known and show that they are human.

Some companies enhance their picnics by having them in special settings like amusement parks. If you do this, consider providing company tee shirts or ball caps to all your people...and perhaps their families. You can imprint them with your company name or logo, and perhaps the date and location of your picnic. Imagine the impact on your people, and others, as you all move around through the entertainment facility in your identical shirts.

There are many more ideas you can use to bring people together. Depending on your company and your people, you can arrange theatre parties, progressive dinners, brown-bag lunches in the office, continuing education lectures or seminars, and other activities. The objective is to bring people together as *people* to enable them to build relationships that will facilitate them working together in their official company roles.

Strategy 7.25
Care about people as individuals.

Each of the people working with you is an individual. While they think of themselves as part of the organization, their first self-descriptors will focus on themselves as individuals.

As human beings, each of us wants to have our own identity. We want to be special, different from everyone else. We want to be recognized for who we are, personally, not just as part of some larger group. Most of us don't like anonymity. We don't want to just blend in.

Get to know your people so you can relate to them on a personal, one-to-one basis. Learn something about their background, their interests, their families, their ambitions. Understand what makes them unique and special.

Use your knowledge of your people to interact with them as individual human beings. Talk with them about their families, their personal interests.

When people accomplish things in your company, reward them as individuals. Extend that individual attention even when you are recognizing group performance. The two levels of attention are not incompatible. You can encourage team performance and salute personal achievement at the same time.

Provide opportunities for people to assert their individuality. These expressions may include freedom in decoration of work areas, business cards for people who don't normally carry them, and name signs hanging over machines in a production area.

Strategy 7.26
Be accessible.

An oft-heard complaint is that managers are not accessible to their subordinates. Part of the problem is real and part of it is perception.

A primary concern is the manager's attitude, and how that attitude is expressed to others. Do your people believe that you hide from them, that you deliberately try to be hard to find? How much is true, and how much is perception?

If your people don't see you on some kind of a regular basis, they may assume that you are avoiding them. It's a legitimate perception; there are managers who want to have little to do with their people and practically hide from them. The attitude and expectation can easily affect people's thinking, even if it is not the actual situation at their company. Just *hearing* that some managers behave that way creates certain expectations.

An open door policy is fine, *if* people feel comfortable coming to your office. Employees in many organizations are intimidated by the boss's office. This might be the case in your company if offices are not easy to get to, if secretaries screen employee visitors and may act as a barrier, or if people are not familiar and comfortable with the managers' offices. Getting into the boss's office should not be difficult.

Have employees in your company been in the management offices? Surprisingly, in many companies the offices are off-limits to non-office personnel. This was the case in an organization where I took over as Chief Executive Officer. I let it be known that employees were welcome in my office. For a solid week, people came to see me, just to have the experience of going into the CEO's office. They really didn't have anything to see me about; they just wanted to see what the office looked like, and if they could actually get in.

To build the comfort level of people coming to your office, invite your employees to visit in your office on a routine basis. Hold meetings and discussions in your office with the involvement of people from throughout your organization. The more comfortable it becomes, the less people will be intimidated when you call them in for an uncomfortable serious conversation.

Even taking these steps might not be effective enough for you. In your organization it might be more appropriate to take your "open door" to your people. Go to where your people are working and communicate with them on the job. Break through formality so your team members feel more comfortable talking with you. Listen carefully to what they have to say. Follow through promptly with whatever actions may be necessary to respond to expressed concerns.

Depending on your environment, there may be other things you can do. One approach might be to spend an entire lunch hour just sitting in the company cafeteria. Invite people to join you and talk informally. If you can do this on some sort of periodic basis, your people will look for you and take the initiative to join you if they have something to say.

Some executives schedule regular meetings with their staff just to listen to what they have to say. Dedicated employees want staff meetings where they can voice their concerns and where they can get some sort of response. These meetings don't have to be formal, just provide an opportunity to talk and listen.

Think creatively to find other ways you can be more accessible to your people. Opportunities will vary from company to company. Seek those solutions which are best for your circumstances.

Strategy 7.27
Have a sense of humor.

"Take your work seriously, but don't take yourself too seriously."

This old adage is meaningful for us in today's working environment. We have to take what we do seriously. With the "lean machine" staffing philosophy in most companies, everyone has a significant amount of important work to do.

However, we can have fun while we work. Happy, relaxed employees are more productive. They work well in an environment with less stress and the enhanced comraderie. Most people are basically happy and positive, enjoying life. The same feelings should be experienced at work.

Unfortunately, many employers do not condone their people enjoying their time at work. The emphasis is placed so heavily on production that employees are made to feel more like robots unemotionally plodding through their workday. The understandable expectation is that work will not be an enjoyable experience, and therefore many people do not look forward to going to their place of employment.

Enlightened companies can break through this barrier of negativity by making work more fun. As employers and managers show their sense of humor and encourage enjoyment of working together to accomplish results, employees will develop better attitudes toward their jobs. As a consequence, absenteeism will drop and productivity and job satisfaction will rise.

When people enjoy their jobs and the positive companionship of the people they work with, they will be more likely to remain with the employer who fosters those special benefits.

How can you make work more fun? The opportunities are limitless. First, enjoy doing your own work and being with the people on your team. If you don't enjoy what you're doing, your people will know this. Your attitudes will affect their attitudes more quickly and more deeply than you might suspect.

If you hear a good funny story, share it with your people. Find the right time and place to do this. While some people might benefit from having their work interrupted for a laugh break, others might prefer to share the laugh during a break or at lunch. Be careful to tell "clean" jokes. While they may laugh out of courtesy, many people are embarrassed and uncomfortable hearing "dirty" jokes.

Celebrate birthdays, promotions, and other special events with short parties. Lunch together with fellow workers, a piece of cake, sharing the moment builds teamness and positive feelings about work. Inexpensive funny gifts can add a lot toward the enjoyment. The celebrations do not have to be long at all; just a short period of fun together can go a long way.

I know of a couple of companies that have monthly get-togethers of almost *all* their employees. One or two people cover the phones while everyone else gathers to share cake and punch or coffee. One company combines celebration of the month's birthdays and employment anniversaries. The company president takes a few minutes to give a brief report to all assembled about company progress. Cost is low, lost production time is minimal, and the building of morale is noticeable.

Balloons are a popular way of recognizing a celebrant. The old-fashioned rubber latex balloons or the foil balloons can be attached to someone's desk or work station in areas where safety is not a factor. The recipient can take the balloons home to share with the family if desired. Fresh flowers can serve the same purpose, as can silk flowers or planters.

Strategy 7.28
Set an example.

The people who work for you look to you as a role model. If you're a leader, by position or relationships, others see you as something special. They will watch your actions and reactions and will follow your lead.

If you are enthusiastic, your people will be enthusiastic. If you are angry, your people will be angry. If you wear nice clothes to work and have a smile for everyone, others will follow your lead. More than you realize, you set the tone for your organization.

To enable people to excel, to be highly productive, and to feel good about themselves and their employer, you need to exemplify those behaviors and attitudes. Alert, loyal team members mirror their leaders. Even those who march to the beat of their own drum are influenced by the way you perform. Without realizing it, many of these people will emulate those they respect and admire.

Assuming people want to achieve, we can appreciate why dedicated workers desire high performance, results-oriented managers and supervisors. Unwittingly, we follow the example of those above us--in position, achievement, seniority, age, and other categories. You set the pace for your team.

If you are in a leadership position, you are being observed more than you realize. People watch the way you walk, talk, and treat others. They note the clothes you wear and how you wear them. They see the car you drive, observing cleanliness, maintenance, and driving habits. Your actions, and reactions, are seen, along with the way you treat your peers, customers, superiors, and subordinates.

Live each day as if you were influencing the lives of all the people with whom you come in contact. You probably are having a significant impact without being conscious of the messages you send every day.

Strategy 7.29

Show leadership at the top of your organization.

A great many people want to be led, or at least guided, by the leader of their organization. While people look to a variety of intermediate leaders to set an example, they look to the *senior* leader(s) to provide leadership and direction.

The top people play a vital role of forward looking leadership in our companies, governments, educational institutions, non-profit organizations and other groups. Senior leaders set the direction and pace for the entire team. It is not a role that can be delegated or abdicated; the responsibility "goes with the territory" of chief leader.

Intentionally or unintentionally, when you're at the top, you are watched by everyone below you. When you're at the head of the line, everyone is following your lead. It's an unavoidable obligation. People depend on their leaders to show the way.

If there isn't someone to show the way, people feel as though they are adrift at sea in a rudderless ship. They're at the mercy of the currents of life, with no control over their own destiny. No one wants to be in that kind of position, so those who perceive their circumstances to be like that rudderless ship will abandon ship.

Executives who want their good people to stay with them have to demonstrate, continually, that they have a firm hand on the wheel...and the throttle. If people don't see that control and focus, their confidence in their leadership begins to erode. If not stemmed by middle managers and front line supervisors, the erosion will affect good people at all levels of the organization with potentially damaging consequences.

Senior leaders must assure that they exert deliberate, visible guidance and inspiration for their followers. Just as important, executives must communicate the exercise of their leadership to all the people in their organization. The guiding presence has to be felt by everyone.

You can show your leadership presence by practicing the now-familiar "Management by Walking Around" technique of being seen in all areas of your organization. Carefully listen, observe, and talk with your people. Keep your comments general enough that you avoid violating the principles of the chain of command. Be seen often in places other than your office. Something as simple as having lunch with your people will give them an opportunity to see their leader in *their* environment.

Share your vision with your people, particularly your direct reports. Be open to their input, but understand that you are expected to make the ultimate decisions about organizational direction. Within the guidelines you set, your people can create, produce, and excel. Your job is to keep their energies focused on what your organization is expected to accomplish.

Strategy 7.30
Reduce stress. Keep anxiety to stay sharp.

Psychologists tell us there are two kinds of stress, negative stress and eustress ("good stress"). Everyone is under stress, since there is some level of tension in everything we do, in every aspect of our lives. The only human body without stress is a corpse.

Eustress is the stress we experience through the positive events in our lives, such as marriage, job promotion, wearing a new outfit, taking a vacation, or winning the lottery.

Negative stress, what we usually mean when we use the word "stress," is what we feel when things are not going well. Causal experiences include divorce or other family problems, trouble at work, an accident, or a flat tire when we're late for an appointment.

To maximize productivity and to keep good people sharp, there should be a positive stress in the organizational environment. Where eustress is seen working for company achievement, we see a sense of competition with another company or with previous accomplishments. We see a desire to lead in a chosen field of endeavor. Tight schedules, close tolerances, and high levels of customer service can be sources of pride and excitement for employees.

Good people usually work well under some sort of eustress. If the feeling does not already exist in the company, these people may create it for themselves. We have all heard about those folks who "work best under pressure" and those who are out to prove something. They build a positive anxiety that empowers them to produce more.

Many good employees, found in sales, research and development, and aggressive management positions, want to be on the cutting edge. They want to be where the action is, making those important footprints in the sands of time. They want to do something significant; for themselves, for their employer, for their profession, for their industry, for society. If you can create and maintain the kind of environment that will encourage and support their endeavors, you can attract and keep these valuable employees.

Those who concern themselves with accuracy, quality, correctness, and detail are also valuable members of your team. They don't necessarily want to be the movers and skaers in their field, but they are usually proud to be supportive of organizations that are striving to make a difference. Their role is to be sure that the company's important work is being done properly. A different kind of environment may be needed to hold these people.

The environments desired by the movers and shakers and by the controllers are not incompatible. You may have to act as an interpreter once in a while to help different kinds of people understand each other. The sense of positive anxiety, the desire to do the right things, the right way, can be a powerful motivational force.

Strategy 7.31

Don't question or second-guess your people all the time.

Good people enjoy a feeling of independence in their work. They want to be entrusted with an assignment or a role and left alone to get the job done. These folks want others to rely on their expertise, their experience, and their personal motivation for accomplishment.

When you give them an assignment or a role to play, good people will usually move forward deliberately to achieve the expected objectives. They want to be left alone along the way. When a superior, or even a peer, continually questions what they are doing, they may feel an erosion of trust from others. This relationship is, at the least, counterproductive. At the most, it can be irritating enough to drive a good employee away.

If you are the kind of boss who wants to know what's going on, what progress is being made, help your good people understand this. Ask them to keep you informed and explain that you may ask some questions to increase your awareness of their work. Do this in a positive way, rather than in a way that suggests you don't trust them to work alone (without your advice/control).

Good people feel they are competent in their work. They can get the job done if just left alone. If you are looking over their shoulder too much, they may be "turned off" and tend to seek other employment opportunities. If they discover you are second-guessing them by following up on their work, doing the same things, or checking too much (in their opinion), they may feel a lack of trust or lack of autonomy. This creates a discomfort that leads to a search for greener pastures.

If you don't trust your people, you may have problems deeper than we can address in this book. If you do trust your people, but just want to know what's going on, share your interest with them. Unless they are hiding something, most good people will be happy to share their efforts with you.

Strategy 7.32
Be firm and fair.

Good people want to be treated fairly, and they want to know that others are also treated fairly. At the same time, they expect those charged with leadership to be firm in enforcing company policies and organizational standards.

Fairness means open, honest dealings with each other. It means equitable treatment of all members of a group, whether that be a group of employees, customers, or suppliers. This doesn't mean that everyone has to be treated the same; it means that everyone has an equal opportunity for accomplishment and that standards are applied in an objective, even-handed manner.

Firmness is equally important. If circumstances call for definitive action to be taken with an employee, customer, or supplier, the action must be taken. Good people do not expect their leaders to be wishy-washy. They want to know where people stand; they must be able to depend on that standing to be firm and reasonably unwavering.

This doesn't mean that there may not be exceptions to the rules. However, exceptions should not become the norm. Good people desire the organization's managers to have strength, internal fortitude to see that things are done, the plans made are followed through. When there are tough decisions to be made, good people expect them to be made--even if those decisions may be unpopular. Good managers are expected to "bite the bullet" when necessary.

To be firm and fair, there will be times when your difficult decisions will produce uncomfortable consequences...at least in the short run. Good people will understand and appreciate the situations. They may not fully support your position, but they will lose confidence in you if you don't do what you have to do.

The same conditions apply with the "good" decisions. When there are exciting opportunities open to the company, good people will expect you to accept the challenge and the risk. After fairly evaluating the consequences, make a firm decision and stick with it.

Good people appreciate leaders who will "face the music" in any kind of situation. Their environment becomes one of clarity and almost predictability. The alternative, capricious and arbitrary reactions to changing conditions, unsettles many good people. An anchor of stability provides a calming effect that enables good people to create and produce without an undue amount of distraction or worry.

Chapter 8

Task Focused Strategies

Much of the attention of your people is focused on task responsibilities. The thirty strategies in this chapter address task-oriented concerns. If people feel positively about their actual work, they will be more comfortable remaining with their employer.

Strategy 8.1
Give people real work to do.

People really don't like "busy work" very much. They much prefer to be engaged in some sort of *productive* work that makes a contribution to the overall results the company is trying to achieve.

Each of your people wants to feel valuable to the organization. That value is derived from what the employee does to help the organization achieve its goals. The more you can link each task to productive mission-oriented results, the more valuable the employee will feel.

To overcome the depreciating impact of busy work, you can attack the problem from two perspectives. First, strive to schedule work so your people can maximize their productive activity on the job. Second, recognize the value of what may be perceived as busy work, giving it a level of importance higher than just stalling or killing time.

No one likes to "hurry up and wait" in their work. In your scheduling, avoid pushing people to the point that they have a period of downtime while they are waiting for others to catch up to them. Try to balance the work among people and among departments so people can pace themselves better.

To overcome this problem, plan the so-called busy work tasks ahead of time. Don't just look around at the last minute for something to keep someone occupied. Have a deliberate system of specific tasks to be done in time available. Make these responsibilities part of the employee's job, individually or as part of a team assignment.

One kind of task that is considered busy work by many employees is cleaning up and straightening merchandise, tools, inventory, or what-have-you. Unless that work is the employee's primary responsibility, your team member may feel that such tasks are inappropriate extra busy work that you are dumping on them just to keep them working.

In actuality, most employees are usually so busy fulfilling the primary functions of their jobs, they have little time left to straighten up or clean up. That kind of work is put off or ignored until it becomes a relatively serious, noticeable problem. It becomes a nuisance, rather than an integral part of the job.

Make these tasks part of the job; with a lower priority perhaps, but still part of the job. Whenever the employee has time available, attention and effort should automatically be directed to the secondary tasks. Make this clear to the employee, placing a value on the non-primary tasks that also have to be accomplished.

For example, a clerk in a retail store has a primary responsibility to serve the customers. However, when there are no customers to be served at a given moment, the clerk should automatically straighten stock on shelves, replace purchased merchandise, and perform similar tasks to present the right kind of buying environment for the next customer.

"Condition" your people to look for things to do when they have some time available. Give them ideas, perhaps a list of what they might do. As you build the team feeling in your organization, people will be more and more willing to pitch in. In many cases, they can help a fellow employee catch up on a work overload. Encourage this kind of effort; praise it whenever you see it.

A side comment: when work is caught up, there are times when it is wise just to let someone take a break and relax for a few minutes. It is not necessary for people to "push" every minute of the work day. In fact, balancing breaks with work, especially when the balance is maturely employee-controlled, gives the mind and body a break and enables people to become even more productive overall.

Strategy 8.2
Provide challenges.

People like to be mentally and/or physically challenged at work. They like to "stretch" beyond the norm. There's a certain excitement about doing something that hasn't been done before, or expanding existing limits, or improving efficiency.

Interestingly, many workers would create their own on-the-job challenges and stretch themselves...if they knew it was permissible or desired. Some employees can't visualize and pursue challenges on their own because they are not able to grasp the "big picture" of the company's mission and the value of their role.

You, as the leader, may have to create and design the challenges that will stimulate your people to stretch for higher achievement. In some cases, this will be a cooperative adventure with your team members; in other cases you will have to show others the path and encourage them to take the steps to walk that path.

Without putting them down by making them feel they are not doing their jobs, show your people there is more they can do. In your communication with them, describe the acceptance and meeting of new challenges in positive terms.

Don't make challenges too big. Experience has shown that the most progress is made in small steps. Seek little improvements that eventually add up to great strides. People are naturally overwhelmed by goals that are too big to understand and achieve. Help people make incremental improvements, getting a little better each day. It's better to have small successes than a big failure.

Strategy 8.3
Fight frustration.

One of the reasons that people leave one employer to go to another is to escape an intolerable level of frustration.

High performers don't mind obstacles and challenges; in fact, they often welcome them. The problem arises when they can't overcome those obstacles and challenges because of frustrations they encounter in the workplace.

One frustration that becomes so irritating that it chases away good people is a lack of cooperation from fellow workers--especially management. People want and need support to get their jobs done. When they don't get it, and don't understand why, the frustration level can build.

The solution obviously is to assure that the support is provided, or that your team member is told why a certain kind or level of support is not available. To be sure that you are aware of the expectations and their level of fulfillment, ask questions. No, I don't suggest you ask your people how frustrated they are! Instead, ask what else *you* can do to support them so they can get their jobs done. What else do they need? How can you help?

Another source of frustration is ignorance--a lack of the information needed to get the job done. People may need information from somewhere else in your organization, from outside your organization, of from some sort of creative process. Stay alert to possible ignorance irritants and work with your people to overcome them as well as you can. Again, when it is difficult to solve the problems for some reason, keep your people advised.

Uncertainty is frustrating. When people are not sure what is going to happen, they are cautious, concerned, and feel as though they are not on firm footing. If other employment opportunities are offered, people experiencing uncertainty are vulnerable to being attracted away from you.

The very nature of doing business in today's world is, in itself, uncertain. People in leadership positions are more accustomed to dealing with uncertainty as a "given" than are the people working as part of their teams. Leaders take it for granted, often assuming that their people regard the frustrating condition the same way.

It's wise to help others put uncertainty in perspective. It's easier to understand and accept the situation as a part of corporate life when you see the big picture. Whenever possible, reduce uncertainty by giving people clear answers about matters that concern them.

Whenever you make changes in your organizational structure, modify your product/service offering, alter your marketing direction, or initiate other changes, expect your people to be uncertain and unsure until you tell them what is happening and how it affects them and what they are doing. People will be concerned for their jobs, for the nature of the work they will be expected to perform, and for the security and future of their employer.

Your people may be subject to other frustrations such as having to fight traffic to get to work, dealing with a recalcitrant phone system, or trying to get things done with equipment that won't function properly. Be sensitive and responsive to these issues.

Strategy 8.4
Remove barriers to task accomplishment.

One of the ways you can keep your good people happy and productive is to remove the barriers that inhibit them from completing their tasks. Remember that most people honestly want to accomplish things at work. When they are not able to achieve that completion, they feel they are lacking something.

Removing barriers may involve a number of different kinds of interventions. With so many variables in the work that people do, we can not possibly list every barrier and intervention. We can, however, address some of the most common.

One barrier that irritates good people is supervisors who don't seem to care. People want support and dedication from their supervisor. Studies have shown that many hourly workers perceive their supervisors as being more concerned for themselves than for their people or for the job that has to be done.

Another barrier cited is managerial indecisiveness. It seems that many companies are plagued by supervisors and middle managers who can not, or will not, make day-to-day decisions.

Hourly workers, and other types of employees in American companies complain that their superiors don't listen to them. The people on the front line see ways that things can be done better, but no one will listen when they try to bring about needed changes. Eventually, these "blocked" employees feel that company leadership really doesn't care. And, if management doesn't care, why should anyone else?

These are only a few of the obstacles that productive employees feel they have to struggle to overcome. Learn what your people are doing...and are not doing. Listen carefully to what they say, staying ever-alert for the identification of perceived barriers. Then work quickly and diligently to remove those barriers so that your people can be, and feel, successful.

Strategy 8.5

Adjust jobs to fit strengths, abilities, and talents.

Few people like to fit into boxes created by others. We like to have some control over our environment, over the way we do things, and over our destiny. Many jobs can be modified to respond to the person filling the position. Employers would be wise to be flexible, allowing employees to make the adjustments that will enable them to make a greater and longer contribution.

Each person has a unique set of knowledge, skills, abilities, attitudes, and talents. Each of your good people brings a special combination to you. To best utilize these resources, allow the employee to modify the way a job is done to suit his/her preferences.

As you design or re-design a job, consider the person now performing the tasks. How can you take advantage of that person's strengths? Are there other jobs that can/should be restructured in your organization? Are the various functions of your company distributed in the most effective way?

You might be able to increase productivity and employee satisfaction significantly by allocating the tasks differently among the members of your team. The happier people are with the way work assignments are arranged, especially theirs, the more likely they are to remain in that employment situation.

Strategy 8.6
Empower people to work as a team.

While many good employees can, and do, work just fine independently, the work to be done today often is best accomplished by two or more people working together as a team. Even work that can be done by one person can be done with more enjoyment, faster, more efficiently, or more effectively when done in partnership with someone else.

Human beings naturally enjoy work and social relationships with others. The joint efforts can be quite productive, while building important bonds among fellow employees.

Is your work environment, physically, functionally, and psychologically conducive to people working together? If it is not, you might want to make some adjustments to facilitate a team working pattern.

We have seen businesses with very small offices or cubicles for key employees. The space is so small and cramped, there is no room for an extra chair for a second employee to sit down and discuss a project with the occupant.

If people want to talk with each other about a shared interest regarding their work, where can they do it? Are conference rooms available? How heavily are those rooms booked with formal meetings that can't be disturbed so a couple of people can sit down and discuss a timely issue?

By not providing floor space, furniture, and supportive arrangements (such as privacy, flip charts, tables to spread papers), you may be sending clear messages to your people that you don't want them to collaborate. If they become less productive because they aren't communicating with each other, take a critical look at what you are doing to encourage or discourage people working together.

Do your managers know how to supervise teams of people? While we find that supervisors can often do fairly well in coordinating and supporting groups of workers or building productive one-on-one relationships, they often fall short in the vital skills of team-building.

Let your people know you like them to work together. Tell them you are anxious for them to strengthen creative problem solving by working more with their colleagues. Support the two-heads-are-better-than-one approach, providing semi-structured opportunities for people to interact, share, and cooperate to get even better results.

Strategy 8.7
Mickey Mouse should be fun, not fundamental.

Good people become quickly frustrated by "Mickey Mouse" rules, regulations, and procedures. People don't want to put up with nonsensical rules and regulations.

Take a good look at your policies and procedures. Look for anything that might call for extra paperwork, unnecessary steps, superfluous approvals, or similar nuisances.

Slash red tape. Destroy burdensome bureaucracy. Cut the harnesses. Get the clutter out of the way. Remove anything that may be an obstacle to the effective and efficient operation of your business.

Do whatever you need to do to make it easy for your people to get things done. Your streamlining efforts will probably make it easier for your customers to do business with you, too.

Strategy 8.8
Keep the promises you make.

This seems basic, doesn't it? It's one of those "of course" things in our lives.

In our work, we've found that countless employees don't feel they can trust their employers to follow through on the promises they make. This is, quite naturally, unsettling for good employees who are trying to help their employer succeed.

Be alert to the effect your seemingly minor actions have on the rest of your organization. When you make a promise, even an announcement of the way things will be done differently, people expect to be able to rely on that statement as true.

If and when you have to change course from what your people are expecting, explain the change to them. If you don't properly convey the reasons for the change, they may perceive you as going back on your word. If this happens too often, you could lose credibility with your people.

Loss of credibility usually leads to loss of loyalty, which leads to the loss of your good people.

Strategy 8.9
Provide the resources to get the job done.

To support your people in the accomplishment of their work, provide all the resources they need to get their jobs done. If it is not possible to furnish the full complement of resources your people feel they need, help them understand what they do have to work with and why they can not have more.

Part of the frustration felt by good people trying to do their jobs comes from not having the resources they want. They may want more people, more or different equipment, more space, more time, or bigger budgets. If they don't get the resources they want, they feel a lack of support from management and wonder whether management really cares and wants them to perform well.

Resources are scarce today, as they always have been in prudent organizations. While we have to make do with what we have, people feel better about it if there is a clear understanding of the situation.

Furnish your people with all the resources you *can* provide to support their efforts. Then, take the time to explain why they can not have more resources. If it is possible for them to trade one kind of resource for another, perhaps with another department, help them understand their capacity to manage their limited pool of resources.

When people understand what they have to work with, and why, they become more focused on achieving the best utilization of those resources instead of complaining that they don't have more.

It is important for managers to understand the relationship between the available resources and the job to be done. If the task simply can not be done with the resources, don't expect the impossible. Unrealistic demands will turn off good people and send them fleeing to organizations led by more reasonable employers.

When people are given all the resources possible, and enabled to understand the big picture, they can often "work miracles" in task accomplishment. Remember that the package of resources you give your team members includes information and perspective.

Strategy 8.10
Avoid rejection, raw criticism, humiliation.

Be sensitive to the way you treat your people. When you are not satisfied with their performance, let them know. But, convey your message with sensitivity to the other person's feelings. Don't put others down deliberately and maliciously. It's not good in the short run or in the long run.

People resent being chewed out by an angry boss, even in private. As much as possible, contain your anger and irritation, communicating with less emotion than you might really feel. Avoid personal attacks and damning terminology. Don't humiliate your people.

Criticize constructively, recognizing the positive attribute of the employee as well as the difficulties. Allow people to save face whenever possible. Build people up; don't tear them down.

When you are critiquing performance of a particular task, focus your remarks on the task itself. Don't allow yourself to be drawn into other aspects of the employees or their work. Talk about how the task could be done differently so your expectations will be met.

Strategy 8.11
Encourage and welcome new ideas.

In the day-to-day operation of our businesses, there will always be ways we can improve what we are doing. The people with the best ideas are usually those directly involved with the tasks that are targets for improvements.

Let your people know that you are receptive, even eager, for their ideas on how things could be done better. Show your interest in ways to serve customers, earn a stronger market share, improve operating procedures, create a safer work environment, or save money.

When ideas are suggested, give each of them your serious attention. Investigate them, consider them, and implement them whenever appropriate. When you move forward with an employee's idea, be sure to give credit where credit is due.

Give the suggesting employee a timely response regarding the disposition of the idea. If it takes extra time to do research before deciding to implement the idea, let the employee know what you're doing. If you can't use the idea, tell the employee and explain why. When people try to help and don't get any feedback, they naturally assume that management doesn't really care anyway. That's the kind of attitude that starts people thinking of leaving a place where they're not appreciated for their ideas.

Many companies have active suggestion programs, with a wide variety of incentives offered to employees for making suggestions. These incentives include cash, certificates, inscription of their name on a plaque, a special parking space, dinner for two, and a chance to manage the implementation of the suggestion. Consider what reward(s) might be appropriate and tell your people about the opportunity to benefit tangibly from their contribution.

Good people have lots of ideas about how things might be done differently. Some of the ideas may be "off the wall" and not really worthwhile. However, it's important to appreciate the effort, the thought, and the willingness to share to stimulate the offering of more suggestions. Be sure to thank people *whenever* they offer a way to improve what the company is doing. Their involvement is valuable.

Strategy 8.12
Define responsibilities.

Good people leave organizations when they don't have a clear idea of their responsibilities, or of their area of responsibility. Clear assignments and recognition are needed if people are to be comfortable with what they are expected to do. Ambiguity fosters uneasiness, which encourages people to look for opportunities with clearer definition.

Responsibilities can be defined at three levels: role, project, and specific task. In order to perform as expected, people need to have their responsibilities clearly defined by their superiors, as well as by their co-workers.

There are responsibilities inherent in the roles we play in organizations. A manager has certain responsibilities that go with the job. To fulfill a role properly, one must establish and maintain certain relationships, behave in a certain fashion (sometimes on and off the job), and be concerned with certain aspects of the company's operation. The responsibilities of the role may not be obvious, especially to someone new to the organization or in the case of a developing organization. They have to be explained and discussed.

When we work with others on a team, to accomplish a specific project or a stream of project-like task groupings, we assume responsibilities as part of that team. Usually a team effort involves a number of responsibilities that have to be assumed by the members of the team. The clearer the definition of those responsibilities, and who is involved with the discharge of those responsibilities, the more productive will be the team.

Project responsibilities are defined by members of the project team, by their designated and/or chosen leader(s), and by people or "forces" outside the team. Sometimes an outside person, perhaps a superior in the organization, assigns responsibilities on the project team. Those responsibilities must be accepted by the individual members, either as assigned or as reallocated internally by the team. Regardless of the process involved, all responsibilities must be recognized by one or more members of the team.

There are specific tasks to be accomplished in all organizations. Responsibilities for those tasks must be clearly defined and communicated to the individuals concerned. Be sure you are clear about who is to do what. If assignments and expectations are not clear, people will tend to blame each other, or outsiders, for incomplete or improper task completion.

To avoid finger-pointing and buck-passing, communicate clearly to others. Ask those accepting assignments of responsibility to explain to you what they understand their responsibilities to be. When you have conscious agreement, you have a significantly better chance of getting your desired results. At the same time, those charged with specific responsibilities will feel better because of their clear understanding.

Strategy 8.13
Define accountabilities.

Accountability is important in today's organizations. It's a concept we'll hear a lot more about in years to come. Not only are enlightened employers trying to push accountability downward in their workforces, but an increasing number of employees want to have a clear idea of exactly what they are accountable for.

People who produce (your good employees) want to be able to stand up and be counted. They want to be recognized, by their superiors, their team members, and/or their professional colleagues for what they accomplish. When they have done something worthwhile, when they have met a challenge successfully, they want to feel legitimate pride that they got the job done.

When you assign a responsibility to someone, assign the accountability for results at the same time. Emphasize the agreement that the person accepting the *responsibility* also accepts the *accountability* for getting the job done correctly and on time. Define clearly what is expected and when it is expected. When you remove the ambiguity, the uncertainty, people are more comfortable because they understand their role.

Good, dedicated employees are willing to accept the consequences, good or bad, of their efforts. If they do well, they want to be rewarded for their achievement. If they do not meet expectations, they are prepared to take the blame. Realizing that their names and reputations are on the line, good people will perform to meet or exceed expectations.

Strategy 8.14
Define authority.

Employees need certain authority to get their jobs done. That authority may include access to information, control of budget dollars or other resources, or freedom to design how a job will be done. If you expect people to perform to their capacity, you have to give them the authority to do what is necessary to produce.

Authority is power. People work best when they have the power to make decisions. They want the power to take a project and follow it through to completion. While they realize that superiors must be kept informed, they thrive when they have the control to use their best judgment to get the results desired.

Power, and thus authority, is carefully controlled in many organizations. Sometimes this control is justified; in other cases, the tight control is a consequence of earlier non-participative management style or a byproduct of people not being able to handle the power. If employees lack the experience or the maturity to use the power properly, the company should monitor its use.

Define what power the employee has...as a member of your team, as someone assigned to a particular project, as the person responsible for specific results. Explain how the power is to be used, and any cautions that may be appropriate.

Ask the empowered employee to check back with you in any situations that may be "borderline" or doubtful. When your guidance is requested, grant as much authority to the employee as you can. This will encourage and motivate people to stretch for you as you have stretched for them.

Strategy 8.15
Encourage initiative.

Initiative can be defined as people doing things before they are asked or directed to do so. It means operating on one's own without having to be told to do something.

Most managers in business today would love to see their employees take more initiative. A few are concerned about the employees going overboard, but most would much rather have to step in and set limits than worry about establishing parameters ahead of time.

Good people want to take initiative. Unfortunately, they are often hampered by their employers, or at least by their superiors. Quite often, the people perceived as standing in the way are the same ones who want their people to take initiative.

So, where's the problem?

The answer is alarmingly simple. Managers unwittingly send messages to their subordinates telling them not to take initiative. No, they don't say it directly, but indirectly the message is received.

Three beliefs must be present before people will take initiative: they must believe they have the *responsibility*, the *authority*, and the *accountability* to take initiative. If any of these elements are missing from the subordinate's beliefs, initiative will not take place.

People will be more likely to take initiative if they see that doing so is part of their responsibility. This means the leader must tell each and every team member that he/she has a responsibility to take initiative. That responsibility must be explained if it is to be understood.

If one of your people takes some initiative on something and gets negative reinforcement from you and/or others, the likelihood of further initiative is significantly diminished. It is vital to give people *positive* reinforcement when they do take initiative, to let them know that you want them to assume responsibilities for things that need to be done, that you appreciate their action.

Do your people have the authority to take initiatives in various aspects of their jobs? Do they know what authority they have, or don't have? Managers have to draw the lines clearly. If the lines of authority are fuzzy, some will opt to stay on the safe side, while others will overstep their authority and potentially cause problems for themselves and you.

Help your team members understand how much authority they have to take initiative without coming to you for confirmation. Let them know that if they come to you with an interest in taking initiate in certain areas, you will probably grant them some special authority to move forward.

A vital issue is accountability. Too many employees do not perceive that they are *accountable to take initiative* in their jobs. "I'm just supposed to do my job" and "They don't pay me to think" are heard too often. You probably need to tell your people, directly, that they are accountable to take initiative if they see something that should be done.

This doesn't mean that workers should go do the tasks assigned to others if they believe the others aren't doing so well. It doesn't mean they should stop doing what they're *expected* to do in their job to take a wide range of initiatives in other aspects of the company's business.

What we do hold people accountable for is taking initiative in their own areas of responsibility. And, if they see something to be done in other areas to communicate that to their supervisor--either for a go-ahead to take the initiative, or for the supervisor to follow through to see that the initiative is taken by someone.

As an example, safety violations are ignored in many organizations because the workers who see them don't take the initiative to correct the problems. They don't see that as part of their responsibility. The supervisors or maintenance should take care of those hazards. Workers don't feel they have the authority to correct safety problems; they anticipate that their supervisor will tell them to get their own job done and not worry about other things. When someone gets hurt, the workers who saw the risk don't feel accountable; management should have done something.

Initiative, with its elements of responsibility, authority, and accountability, rest at too high a level in the organization. They must be pushed downward so people directly involved with accomplishing the day-to-day work feel more a part of the results of their efforts.

Leaders would be well advised to share more responsibility with their people. Workers at all levels should be made more accountable for specific and general tasks and issues. Give more authority to those expected to get the job done.

Strategy 8.16
Inspire and enable creativity and innovation.

Good people thrive in environments where they are encouraged to be creative, to seek new ways of doing things. When such people have the freedom, and the support, to innovate on the job, they are more likely to remain with the employer who provides those opportunities.

Creativity and innovation are not, by any means, limited to the research and development folks. People in accounting may see a way to gather and present information better than it is being done today. They may learn of some new technology and want to apply it to their work.

Truck drivers may see better ways to organize delivery routes to improve efficiency and customer service. Machine operators in production shops may have some ideas about tooling or material flow. Retail clerks may want to create special displays to promote some particular merchandise better. The list can go on and on.

An amazing proportion of employees believe that they are not supposed to be creative. They are not supposed to try new ways of doing things. Innovation is believed to be frowned upon by management wanting everything done the same way all the time. Procedures are seen as being more important than results. The perception is there, but you have the opportunity to change it.

Let your people know that you encourage new ideas. Ask for input from those on the front lines: they often see things more clearly from their perspective. They know what ought to be done, but don't think management wants them to do it. Your efforts can range from an active suggestion box program to giving your people the power to try new methods or approaches.

Many companies have aggressive programs offering cash awards, special parking spaces, recognition, and other incentives to employees making suggestions that are implemented. Actively looking for better ways becomes a part of the corporate culture.

Your suggestion program should at least have a response system so people know someone is seriously interested in hearing ideas. The suggestions made, and management's responses, can be posted on a bulletin board next to the suggestion box. It's important to explain why non-accepted suggestions can not be implemented. Without this feedback, employees may think no one is even reading what they write. It sounds silly to even mention it, but be sure there is an ample supply of suggestion forms available.

Whenever possible, allow and enable people to test their new ideas. This can be done on a formal, planned, budgeted basis. It can also be done on an informal basis with *go ahead and try it* being the ongoing message.

When people try new ideas, there is always the risk of failure. As much as possible, give people *permission to fail* in trying something different. We learn a considerable amount from our mistakes. People don't want to fail, but they will take the initiative to be daring in a new venture if they feel they have support.

Your role as management is to monitor the innovative efforts to limit the risk and/or protect the venture from outside attack. There may be those in your organization who will not be supportive of experimentation. You may need to insulate your innovators from your overly-cautious people. Great companies have been built by daring people; other companies have been ruined by them. Your challenge is to keep the efforts positive.

Do your people believe their employer encourages trying new and better ways to do things? Is the company interested in new products or innovative applications of technology? If there is a question in your mind, ask your people. Then, based on what you learn, communicate appropriately to send or reinforce the message.

Strategy 8.17
Establish limits, parameters.

Good people can be extremely valuable, a positive asset. However, they can also become overzealous and overstep the bounds of sensibility. Unbridled enthusiasm can lead to inappropriate actions that may cause difficulties for the good people and their company.

One of the roles of leadership is to set limits. Let your people know how far they can go. Establish legitimate parameters and your people will operate within them.

The limits do not have to be tight; they can be very broad. They should still be there, so some sort of control is in place. You may never have to exercise that control, but your good people will appreciate knowing that there is some structure to what they are doing.

The best approach seems to be to set wide limits, with lots of flexibility. Give people as much room as you can to operate and to stretch.

Two levels of "limits" seem most effective. The first is the area in which the employee may function without checking with anyone. The second level, beyond the limits of the first, requires the employee to check with management before proceeding.

People really do appreciate knowing their limits. It builds their confidence knowing what freedom they have, but they also like to know that organizational controls are in place.

Strategy 8.18
Know what your people are doing.

In the management of the various tasks to be completed by your organization, it's essential to know what your people are doing.

It usually isn't necessary to know every little detail of what people do each day or each week, but you should be aware of what they are working on, what progress they are making, and what results they are achieving.

There are several reasons for maintaining this knowledge. First, part of your role as a leader is to know what's happening in your organization. Second, this awareness will keep you alert to opportunities for recognition and reinforcement. Third, you will be more sensitive to needs for you to lend support and to share your personal expertise. Fourth, your people will know that you are interested and that you care about what they are doing.

This doesn't mean that you have to be right on top of people all the time. You don't need to know every time they take a deep breath! Based on your people, and the circumstances of your situation, keep abreast of what's happening. While written or oral reports to you on some regular basis will work, your being involved enough with your people will be much more effective.

Good people will usually not mind your wanting to know what's going on. If they object to your inquiries, this may be a warning sign that something is amiss. Usually, good people will appreciate your interest and will want to share (brag?) with you.

Companies lose good people when those high performers don't feel management is really interested in what they are doing. Stay involved, but avoid getting in people's way. It's a fine line to walk; you'll make some mistakes. But, better to err on the side of caring than on the side of being disinterested.

Strategy 8.19

Respond when people ask for approval or guidance.

One of the frustrations for good people is the lack of response or direction they receive from their managers. Some managers believe that good people don't need the hand-holding and personal attention. They do. Your high performers may not need as much attention, nor the same kind of attention, but they need it just the same.

Some of your top people will tell you they don't need to have your approval all the time. It's a matter of pride and self-reliance in many cases. While they may not want the frequent pats on the back, everyone appreciates at least an affirmation from the boss that they're on the right track.

People look for signals from others, particularly their superior and their valued associates, that give them some feedback. When they're doing well, they like to receive some indication of approval and support from others. We all do; it's a natural human need.

You don't have to make dramatic statements and heap praise to convey your message. A simple head nod, smile, a thumbs-up sign, or a few quiet words will often suffice. Be sensitive to the fact that different people will need more "stroking" than others, and tailor your communication to the individual. Additional helpful insight will be found in Appendix A.

Most of your good people can do quite well for a while. Every so often, however, they need some guidance from their manager or other key players about what they're doing. If they are not able to gain clear guidance when they ask for it, dedicated employees can become irritated and anxious. They want to move ahead with their work, but may perceive themselves to be stalled by a lack of responsiveness from someone else.

When high performers, eager to proceed with their work, feel a lack of support, they begin to feel like they are paddling upstream. If you don't respond with answers to questions, approval to move forward, budget support, or whatever is being asked of you, your good people will be more prone to invitations to work elsewhere.

Encourage your people to assert themselves if you are not highly sensitive to what they need from you. Some managers are not as alert as others and need some prodding. Build understandings of how you and your good people will work together so everyone's needs will be satisfied.

Strategy 8.20
Give clear direction.

One of the complaints heard from employees striving to perform well is that their bosses don't give clear directions. They don't explain well enough just what they want so the employees can meet (or exceed) their expectations. Do you fall into this category? At least some of the time?

If you're being totally honest with yourself, you will probably answer affirmatively. Yes, you are guilty of not always giving clear direction to others. Sometimes your team members have to struggle on their own trying to understand just what you mean.

Your team members are probably hesitant to come back to you for clarification. After all, how many people want to tell their boss they're confused?

Do your best to be clear when you tell others what you want them, or the organization, to do. Encourage questions and discussion of your mutual concerns to assure common understanding.

Build the kind of relationship with your people that makes it comfortable for them to come back to you with follow-up questions or related issues.

Avoid being patronizing when you give direction. Appreciate that more than one conversation might be needed to get your message across. Don't put others down for not understanding the first time. Remember, if they did not understand, you failed to communicate.

Giving direction, support, and guidance is an ongoing process. It doesn't just happen once and everyone lives happily ever after.

Strategy 8.21
Get people involved.

People want to feel a part of what's going on in their work function. They want to have a say in what work will be done, the sequence of the work, and how it will be accomplished. They want to have input into changes in their work environment, scheduling, and even the hiring of new employees.

More and more, we're going to find that people want a more meaningful role on the job. This will apply particularly to your better employees; they will have a greater contribution to make and will be even more eager to participate in the decision-making process.

When people want to get involved, and they are not allowed the opportunity, they become alienated toward management and toward the organization. This, obviously, can lead to people leaving the company. For some, being directly involved in the management of their work is highly important.

Soliciting someone's opinion does not necessarily mean you will follow that person's advice or preference. You can show you care by asking for input, but the ultimate decisions are still yours to make. That's part of your job as a manager.

Not every decision you make will be a popular one. You have to rely on your own judgment regarding the best choices to make. Even if you don't select the alternative recommended by your team member(s), your people will appreciate your interest and your receptivity to their ideas. In most cases, you will find they will have a greater tendency to support your decision, whether they agree or not, because they know you gave their input fair consideration.

When you invite your people to contribute their suggestions, ask for the reasons behind their proposals. This will not only give you greater depth for consideration of various alternatives, it will also give you greater insight into the thinking of your people.

There is an almost unlimited number of ways to get people involved. They range from deliberation on a major corporate decision to ideas on the rearrangement of furniture in the office. Take advantage of as many opportunities as you can to offer people a chance to put in their "two cents worth" when there is a decision to be made.

Strategy 8.22
Reduce reporting requirements.

Your good people are probably eager to focus their energy on accomplishing their objectives. They don't want to be burdened with excessive requirements for reporting their progress, their attendance, or the status of their paper clip supply.

The definition of "excessive requirements" for reporting will vary from person to person. The need for information is understood by most high performers, but the process is annoying...or even exceedingly irritating. Be sensitive to the attitudes people have about reporting and make the process as easy and non-interruptive as you can.

Some high achievers don't want to be bothered with any reporting at all. They insist they do not have time for such nonsense; they're too busy getting things done. When you ask for a minimal amount of data for project tracking, for instance, these people may get all upset.

"I don't have time for all this nonsense," they may argue. "Do you want me to get this work done or fill out your *@#!*%# forms?" When such people have calmed down, help them understand why you need information from them. Don't ask for any more than you need; minimize their paperwork burden.

If you can find ways to make the reporting easy for your people, you will earn greater cooperation, more accurate information, and less hassle.

Many managers want to know where their people are and what they are doing. That is a perfectly legitimate expectation, from management's perspective. When you ask for such knowledge, anticipate such reactions as, "Don't you trust me?" and "Do you want me to get the job done or punch a time clock?". Answer these questions for yourself, then explain your position to your people.

Help people understand your position in having to monitor the resources of the organization. Emphasize, as appropriate, the need to know where people are or when they will be in...particularly when people must coordinate with each other in their work. Give people as much freedom as you can, but insist on cooperation in adherence to rules and procedures when you feel it is important for the organization.

Reporting is not limited to attendance, or physical presence in a particular work area. The more significant aspect of reporting involves sharing progress on projects or tasks undertaken. Good managers stay on top of what's happening in their organizations, but they avoid getting involved in a highly detailed tracking system. Keep it simple.

Many high energy workers don't want to take the time to fill out a lot of report forms. Paperwork is the bane of their existence. Limit the forms control for these people, giving them the opportunity to report orally in staff meetings. Many managers hold weekly meetings just to provide a forum for all key people to share what they are working on, what progress is being made, coordination needed with others, and problems encountered.

Some of your good people will enjoy filling out forms or reporting what they are doing. Appreciate that people have different needs (see Strategy 7.1 and Appendix A) and work with them to achieve your best information relationship. You will have to re-focus some of these people from reporting as much as they want to.

For the best use of your time, structure your reporting systems to give you the basic knowledge you need to do your job. No more. Keep everyone focused on the productive nature of information-sharing, for you and everyone else in the organization.

Strategy 8.23
Don't look over people's shoulders.

Your job as a good manager, as a good leader, is to put the best people in the right positions, clarify your expectations, provide the needed resources, and get out of the way.

Your people need several things from you to stay focused on the task(s) at hand:

- trust
- confidence
- space.

Their job includes taking care of the details. The only times you should be involved in their task responsibilities is when they ask for your help or when you are unsure of what they are doing. That uncertainty, which could indicate a lack of trust and confidence, is natural for concerned managers who aren't getting enough of the right kinds of information from their people. (*See Strategy 8.22*)

If your people object to your looking over their shoulders, literally or figuratively, as they work, correct your problem.

If your problem stems from insufficient information about what people are doing, make necessary adjustments in your reporting systems.

If your problem stems from a lack of confidence or trust in people doing the job, determine why you feel that way. If you are concerned about their competence, provide the training and experience to build that competence. Don't expect miracles from people.

Your problem might be that you have too much knowledge, especially compared to your people, about particular tasks. If you had their job before, you may be tempted to jump in and do it again. If you do, beyond an instructional period, your people won't be able to learn to fly on their own. And, you might get so bogged down doing their work for/with them, you won't fulfill your own responsibilities.

If your problem stems from having the wrong people in the job.... take the steps you have to take to have confidence in your people to do their job, then give them plenty of elbow room to do it. Focus on their results, their accountabilities, rather than their specific task activity.

Strategy 8.24
Don't keep people overtime without previous notice.

The dedicated people who produce for your company all day long probably have plans after work. They have family obligations, social engagements, or things they want to do. Their day is planned, with both work and after-work aspects clearly defined. If nothing specific is planned, they may just be looking forward to relaxing after work.

When their supervisor unexpectedly asks them to work over, past the normal ending time of the day's schedule, the change could be disrupting. If they had some advance notice, many of these same people could put in the extra hours with less disruption of their lives.

You will find that a great many of your people will gladly work hard during their scheduled work time, but don't like to change their work hours without some planning. These folks do not like unexpected change and will react against it. They may refuse to work, be less productive or attentive, or just develop a negative attitude about management's lack of planning and organization. Whatever the actual expression may be, the feeling is against the company. This increases the likelihood of these valued employees being receptive to employment opportunities elsewhere.

Plan your work, and the work of your people, to avoid or minimize overtime. This helps control your costs as well as manage the work schedule. If you are already running on a standard schedule of more than forty hours a week, maintain a fixed program as much as possible.

When you do have to extend working hours, to meet customer needs, better manage production flow, or accommodate a project, schedule those additional hours ahead of time. Last-minute, "I-need-you-to-work-over-tonight" arrangements should be the exception rather than the rule.

The more notice you can give your people, the more they will appreciate your consideration. They will probably be more responsive and, consequently, more productive, too. Your advance planning will demonstrate your planning and effective management, enhancing the loyalty and respect your people have for you.

Strategy 8.25
Appreciate routine work.

Workers who want recognition (all of us want to be appreciated) often think they have to do something extraordinary to get attention. Unfortunately, they are usually correct. Most supervisors seem to notice only when people do something exceptionally good or exceptionally bad.

Some of your most valuable people, frequently overlooked, are the folks who come in every day, don't bother anyone, and get their work done in a reliable, routine way. You can depend on them to be productive. They are probably the very foundation of your organization.

Other people on your team may be involved in some special assignment work, but are still counted on to take care of some routine tasks that "somebody has to do" to keep things running.

The performance of that routine work is important to your operations. If it were not done, you could be in serious trouble.

Every once in a while, take time out to thank those people who usually don't get thanked. Show some appreciation for the routine work done by members of your team in addition to the more exciting parts of their jobs.

I vividly remember giving a customer service seminar to employees of a bank a number of years ago. During a discussion of face-to-face encounters with customers who appreciate good service, an accounting clerk exclaimed that what we were talking about didn't relate to her; she never had any communication with the bank's customers.

This triggered my curiosity. In response to my question, this fine lady explained that she worked in a back room keeping records and never talked with any customers. In fact, she rarely had conversations with anyone other than the woman who shared the office with her.

I strode over to her table and, on behalf of all the bank's customers, gave her a little hug and said "thank you." This dedicated employee burst into tears! In all her many years with that employer, that was the first time anyone had ever thanked her!

Make a note: is there someone you want to thank?

Strategy 8.26
Enter into performance contracts.

With the confusion and ambiguity about what performance we expect from our people, a wise technique is to enter into a sort of contract with each of your people.

This does not have to be written. We're not talking about anything formal. In performance contracting, you and your team member agree on what the employee will do "under contract" to you and the organization. In return for satisfactory performance, you will provide compensation in the form of wages/salary/commission, benefits, and various kinds of support. Both parties agree to keep their part of the bargain.

The evaluation of the performance is a constant effort, but is formalized during the periodic appraisal of the employee. Some managers seek other times to talk with the employee about how both sides of the agreement are being fulfilled. You have to do your part, too.

A number of employers encourage (or even require) managers to do various kinds of "contracting" with employees during the official performance appraisals. Both parties agree on performance standards, expected improvement, desired training and education, and career path opportunities.

In some companies, Management by Objectives becomes a tool to establish and maintain performance contracts. This can, in its more formalized application, involve written plans and goals with specific objectives and timetables.

Whether you use an informal conversation, a formalized written program, or something in between, arrive at some sort of agreement with your employees regarding what they will do... and what you will do.

Strategy 8.27
Fight boredom.

Be sensitive to how your people are performing their tasks. Do they stay alert, attentive, interested? Some jobs can get downright boring after a while, increasing the risk of errors, accidents, or dissatisfaction.

Help your people fight boredom in the kind of work that can produce those feelings. One approach is to schedule more frequent breaks for people engaged in monotonous work. Play music with varying beats and sounds, such as that offered by Muzak and similar systems. Give people freedom to take a break away from the work as they need to get away from a tedious job for a few minutes.

A machine shop we know cross-trained a number of their employees in each other's jobs. All of the tasks involved highly routine, boring work. Every couple of hours, the supervisors would have the employees rotate to another kind of work. Everyone shared together, building teamwork, and they relieved each other's boredom by sharing the load of the various routines.

Strategy 8.28
Design tasks to meet personal needs.

Each of us has personal needs and preferences in the kinds of work we do and how we do it. These preferences may be environmental, task-focused, or relationship-based.

Some people prefer to stand when they work; others like to sit. While some people prefer working outside, others want inside jobs. Travel is preferred by some, while others don't want to leave town if they can help it.

There are those folks who like working with their hands, and there are those who prefer work where they thinking or communicating. Some people love to organize projects and make things happen, and they're different than those who want to follow someone else's lead and get tasks accomplished.

Working with people is just what the doctor ordered for many people. But, many other people prefer to work independently, perhaps with little or no contact with others.

As much as possible, tailor the tasks to be done, and the way they are done, to the individual preferences of those who will be performing the tasks. If you can not modify the job sufficiently to respond to the needs and wants of the employee, consider shifting the employee to a different type of work.

The better the match between the worker and the work, the greater the results.

Strategy 8.29
Give people a break.

This may come as a surprise to some old school, hard line managers: people are not machines. They have limitations and they need to be treated differently.

When workloads are heavy and resources like extra people are slim, some companies work their people for days and days without sufficient time off to enjoy a mental and physical break. This can cause dangerous fatigue and stress. Even if your loyal team members want to pitch in to get the job done, don't let them overdo it.

I encountered a company recently that had a considerable number of orders to be filled. With the possibility that the production load was temporary, management did not want to hire more people. Instead, they worked their people as many as seventeen days straight without a day off. You can imagine how those people felt. They were proud, but exhausted.

With the shortage of good people, these circumstances may occur with more frequency than in the past. Resist the temptation to work, work, work. Human beings need a break. They'll return to the job refreshed and more productive.

Strategy 8.30
Give specifics in performance feedback.

Good people want to know specifically how they are doing and how they can improve. Interestingly, many supervisors seem reluctant to be specific, offering generalized feedback and evaluations instead.

As you talk with your employees about their performance, include specific examples to illustrate what you like or dislike about what the employee does. With an understanding of what you want and don't want, your team member can make definitive modifications to satisfy you.

The days of "gee, you're wonderful" performance appraisals are gone in excelling organizations. Today's enlightened managers give their people the information needed to meet expectations. Everyone working for these communicative leaders understands what tasks are to be done, how they are to be accomplished, and when work is to be finished. Employers, managers, employees--everybody wins.

Chapter 9

Compensation Strategies

A principal reason people leave an employer to join another is to gain improved income and/or benefits. This motivation has existed for generations and will continue to be an influence. It's become more significant in recent years with increased mobility and changing social values.

Today, working people want to have something to show in return for their investment of time, thought, and energy. People want money to spend, money to save, and the security and comfort of a reasonably strong benefit program. The younger generations of American workers have become more conscious of conspicuous consumption--showing achievement through the acquisition and display of material goods.

Many of us equate "more" with "better", focusing on the quantity of compensation rather than the quality of the position we hold or the work we perform. For some people, the compensation is the overriding issue; for others, it's a matter of being fairly compensated while enjoying a positive work environment.

Some people look at compensation from a competitive perspective. The level of wages, salary, commision, and bonuses becomes a comparative measure of achievement. The comparisons may be sibling-sibling, neighbor-neighbor, employee-employee, or a variety of other relationships. One can even compare today's compensation package against what was received last year or in a previous job. We need to be sensitive to how our people feel about the competiveness issue and enable them to hold their own in the race.

With varying tax treatment of differing methods of receiving income, cafeteria benefit programs, and a wide range of combinations of compensation elements, employers have a great deal of flexibility. The costs are still there, but today we have more ways to create compensation packages that are practically custom-tailored to the needs of individual employees.

The key to success in this arena is to assure that the way you put things together is both legal and fair to all concerned. Most importantly, from our perspectives in keeping good people, is that the arrangement be good for the employee...*in the perception of the employee.*

Rapid Change

The field of compensation is changing rapidly. Flexible financial packages, combined with creative benefit offerings, are heavily influenced by an ever-changing tax structure. What works today may not even be legal tomorrow. Today, we need compensation professionals to stay on top of the situation.

Because of the speed with which the compensation arena is changing, we will not deal in depth with this topic. While we can talk in general about deferred compensation, salary/bonus ratios, and other approaches, it would be a disservice to our readers to be definitive about compensation issues.

In addition, although compensation is important, the thrust of this book is in a different direction. The philosophy of Keeping Good People is that if the non-monetary strategies are employed, there will be less need for emphasis on the compensation area.

The wise approach to follow in compensation management is to work with professional advisors who stay current with this complicated field. Your accountant, benefits broker, and attorney will be helpful. Depending on your situation, you may want to engage a specialist in compensation to guide you.

Strategy 9.1

Present the full value of compensation.

Show your employees the full value of their compensation package. In our work, we have found that most employees do not really understand the "big picture" of their monetary and non-monetary reward for their work. Enlightened employers are providing employees with detailed information explaining the value of the employer's benefit program.

A typical technique is to list all the benefits available to the employee. Next to each one, show its equivalent dollar value on an annual basis. For example, if you provide health insurance coverage, paying all or part of the cost of this benefit, show the dollar amount you contribute each year. For sick leave, show the amount of money you would have paid for the days available if the benefit were fully used.

Be sure to show the dollar value of your contributions to government-mandated programs such as Social Security, Workers Compensation, and Unemployment Insurance. These vary from state to state, so be sure to adjust your figures to account for differences affecting employees in various locales.

Some companies showing their employees the cost break-down even go so far as to include administrative costs for processing health insurance claims. The rationale is that this would be something the employee would have to do personally (at a time-dollar cost) if individually insured.

The presentation of this individualized report can be done on an annual basis, distributed to all employees at one time. Another approach is to prepare the report on each employee's anniversary date of employment. It can be given to the employee by a supervisor, human resources person, or senior executive. Use your imagination to see how this can be done most effectively in your unique organization.

Strategy 9.2
Provide linking incentive opportunities to all employees.

Growing competitiveness dictates that employees fully understand the role of their job and how it impacts the success of the organization. One method of focusing the attention of all employees on maximizing their performance level is through providing incentive opportunities, at all levels of the organization, commensurate with the employee's level of responsibility or contribution.

Typically, incentive plans will be of different design or emphasis for various levels and job functions in the organization. Some should be based on the accomplishment of key strategies. Others should be based on productivity or task accomplishment as appropriate.

Rewards should be based upon measured results which have been communicated to employees and understood by them. Incentive plans should be designed in such a manner that the incremental reward opportunities link together and are logical, equitable, challenging. Provide outstanding total compensation for outstanding performance.

Designing incentive plans on a unilateral basis insures that individual segments of the organization are not ignored and that all employees feel part of the team.

Strategy 9.3
Link performance with rewards.

Linking pay with performance has long been an objective of compensation plans, but by and large has not been well executed. One of the main reasons that "performance based" plans have failed is that the expectations of employer and employee have not been well matched or managed. To avoid problems with performance based reward systems, no matter if they are incentive-based or merit pay-based, a few sound ground rules should be followed;

- keep the plan simple,
- develop realistic objectives which can be measured to as great an extent as possible,
- define the level of *expected* performance for each objective,
- develop a performance array i.e., what is unacceptable performance, what is expected, and what constitutes outstanding performance,
- get employee "buy-in" or ownership with each objective to insure commitment,
- focus on key issues which truly impact operations, the employee, and the company (usually three to four objectives are sufficient), and
- thoroughly communicate the reward system to employees, describing how it is calculated and how they can impact the outcome of their reward.

Approaching performance pay design with this methodology will insure that there are no reward surprises and that rewards are equitable and motivational.

Strategy 9.4
Leverage the total cash compensation package for maximum effectiveness.

Establishing the basic components of total cash compensation, and the relationship between them, is a critical element to the success of any performance based compensation program, whether it is intended be for executives, salespersons, staff or hourly workers. The two key components, base salary and incentive opportunity, must be set in proper relationship for maximum performance and cost effectiveness.

Base salary levels should be established on the basis of labor market competition, industry competitiveness, internal equity, ability to pay, control of fixed labor costs; and the extent to which incentive opportunities are available.

In some cases an employer will provide only a "living wage" for base salary, but provide an opportunity for a very high level of total cash compensation via incentives. This strategy may be a function of the industry in which the company operates, the way operations are structured, the level of profit margins produced, the amount of labor available, the ratio of material costs to labor, or the degree to which the organization's pay philosophy impacts employee earnings.

In other cases employers will provide a higher ratio of base salary to incentive opportunity. This is more appropriate where the labor force is tight, the product and market more mature, or the margins higher.

Incentive compensation's pay focus today and for the foreseeable future will be on reducing or containing fixed labor costs. For the employee this means only one thing: reduced opportunity for guaranteed increased earnings. For the employer this means a better control of costs, but a reduced opportunity to motivate employees. The solution to this dilemma is through performance - driven incentive opportunities. Both employer and employee win.

The establishment of the level of available incentive opportunity (leveraging) is critical. If employees are to accept a reduced level of base salary, then the incentive must be perceived as a sound opportunity. It must be seen not only as a make up for base salary, but as a real opportunity for outstanding total compensation if performance objectives are achieved. Without the proper leveraging, the motivational intent and potential effectiveness is lost. The level of incentive opportunity should be based upon;

1. age of company (i.e.,new, highly leveraged companies in start-up mode may wish a ratio of lower base, higher incentive),

2. competition,

3. industry practice,

4. motivational stretch required,

5. organizational culture (i.e., participative/ non-participative)

6. pay philosophy.

Strategy 9.5

Design reward systems for employee involvement.

Competition, mergers and acquisitions, cost reduction, organizational structuring, technology and work methods have made it imperative that organizations rethink how they utilize their work forces. These imperatives, when directly faced, demand work forces that are more flexible, responsive, productive, knowledgeable, efficient, and more able to deal with and solve problems at their own work level.

As a result, more and more employers are approaching this need with employee involvement (EI) teams. For many companies these changes mean not only cultural and organizational shock, but substantial changes in their pay schemes to address the new work methods and to retain employees who have become more valuable as a result of these methods.

Group incentives most effectively address the employee involvement concept and will emerge during the 1990's as a significant method of compensation. Group incentives basically fall into two categories: profit sharing and gainsharing.

Although profit sharing has been around for a number of years its popularity and effectiveness as a compensation tool is growing rapidly. The concept is simple, its measures are understandable and it is popular with employees from the standpoint of motivation and retention. Profit sharing plans can be of an immediate cash type or can take the form of a deferral which has tax advantages for the employee and can be used as a retirement supplement. Whether the plans are of a cash or deferred type, the mechanics operate in a similar way.

First, a threshold amount of profit must be achieved, or specific profit reserves set aside, before the plan begins to operate. Next, a set percentage of profits are "banked" or set aside to generate the profit sharing fund. At the end of the performance period, the fund is distributed to employees either directly in cash as a fixed or escalating percentage of base salary or deferred into an employee's account.

If the plan is a deferred type, it may allow for employee deposits as well on a pre-tax and/or after tax basis. The deferred assets are normally invested in one or multiple funds such as diversified funds, guaranteed interest funds, bond funds, company stock funds, real estate funds or life insurance for participants.

Cash plans, which may have a shorter life than deferral plans can be designed to pay off as the company meets certain profit objectives on a quarterly, semi-annual or annual basis. These plans may have formulas or certain individual performance criteria as elements which help determine individual profit sharing awards.

The idea behind the profit sharing concept is that all employees have a hand in helping the organization and should be rewarded in direct relationship with how profitable (or unprofitable) the organization is.

Gainsharing plans are becoming the most rapidly growing plans for rewarding employee groups or employee involvement. Gainsharing plans, profit sharing plans and all their variations fall under the category of non-traditional reward systems. Gainsharing, broadly defined, is any corporate or unit-wide pay plan or system designed for rewarding all participants for improved performance. "Gains", or measured real-dollar savings, are shared with all employees in the work unit according to set formula(s).

In the past, incentive plans have focused on specific segments of the work force. Gainsharing, however, is often based on involving all employees in the unit under the plan. The most prevalent reasons for implementing a gainsharing plan are to improve productivity, improve quality, reduce costs and improve employee relations.

The most prevalent of the gainsharing plans are Scanlon, Rucker, Improshare and cash profit sharing (within a strategic business unit). Recent experience with gainsharing plans has indicated that, in order for them to work most effectively, employee involvement and information sharing is critical. The most prevalent type of payment under gainsharing plans is cash in the form of a separate check. Other organizations include the gainsharing payment in the basic earnings, while still others defer the amount.

As a strategy for keeping good people, gainsharing is an excellent choice, providing the organization's culture promotes employee participation. All employees have a higher stake in the organization and its drive for success. There is a heightened employee commitment to achieving that success and a managed expectation regarding eventual reward.

Strategy 9.6
Compensate high potential/low skill employees with a skills-based system.

One of the dilemmas we will face in the 1990's is the scarcity of skilled workers. This situation dictates that companies will have to seek out those people entering the work force who have high potential, even though they have no demonstrated skills. Once companies have identified and hired workers of this type, they must immediately begin the process of training them in the work ethic and then building their skills.

The compensation strategy must yield more than just a paycheck. It must yield an understanding of the relationship between performance and reward, then stress the element of reward and how it can grow in relationship to the accumulation of skills and abilities. This type of goal in a compensation strategy would give indication that some form of skill-based pay would be effective. A program such as this would recognize both the issues of quantity/quality and the improvement of skill levels, while at the same time lending itself as a basis for participation in incentives as the skill base grows.

Skill based pay systems work best in participative environments and have their roots in the thought that the more employees know about their work, the more productive and valuable they are. Therefore, the greater the accumulation of skills a worker has the more he/she should be paid. Obviously the per-capita earnings under this pay system are high, but are offset by high productivity, high quality, and worker flexibility. Translating this type of system to employees who need skill building presents some definite advantages:

1. There is an opportunity to learn, be productive and be paid for it.

2. The list of skills to be acquired is clear with a direct link between skills acquired and pay.

3. Employees understand what they must do to acquire new skills.

4. Role models and training is available in the work place; and

5. Once one set of skills is acquired and the learning process and work ethic established, employees can acquire new skills and move through the organization more quickly.

Skill-based pay programs are now being tried in office settings as well as on the factory floor. They should prove useful as one of the components necessary to attract, train and retain high potential, low skill employees.

Strategy 9.7
Use flexible benefits in a changing workforce.

The change in the composition of our work force and escalating employee benefits costs has caused employers to take a serious and critical look at the type of benefits they provide, how they provide them, and how the costs for these benefits can be significantly reduced. Companies generally spend in excess of 40% of payroll on employee benefits (including statutory benefits), with health care expenditures comprising a significant portion of recent growth in benefit expenses.

Thirty years ago, benefit plans were designed to meet the needs of the "typical employee" - a man with a wife and children at home. These benefit packages usually included a retirement plan, medical, disability and life insurance, and perhaps some ancillary benefits.

Today, however, that once-typical employee comprises less than 10% of the work force. The remainder is comprised of working couples, with or without children at home, and singles, some with children. At the same time, there is a much higher percentage of females in the work force.

These life-style changes during recent decades have caused employers to reevaluate the need for certain traditional benefits. Traditional benefit packages often do not meet the needs of the majority of employees. Working couples may have duplicate medical insurance, but lack desired coverage for child care. For instance, single employees may have life insurance they do not need or appreciate, but lack disability income they wish they had.

Recent data indicates that only slightly more than half of all employees feel positively about their total benefit package. This is a continuation of a downward trend that began about ten years ago. Much of this drop is due to the fact that many benefit packages have not kept pace with the myriad demographic changes and resulting shifts in benefit needs.

Although most companies have incorporated cost containment provisions into their benefit programs, and the percentage of companies requiring employee contributions to some of their benefits has risen dramatically, these changes have not achieved significant improvement in cost control.

Flexible benefits provide one solution to this dual dilemma. While giving employees options from which they can design their own benefit package, it also puts the employer in a position to control spending. As benefit costs increase from year to year, the employer can decide what portion, if any, of the added cost will be absorbed by the company and what portion will be paid by the employees (usually on a before-tax basis).

In addition to medium-sized and large companies, employers with less than 100 employees can now successfully design and implement a flexible benefits program. While a flexible benefits program may not be suitable in every environment, employers can ask themselves some important questions to help make the right benefits decision for their company:

1. does the company's benefit package provide coverage that some employees do not need or want?

2. are there benefit coverage that could be provided that some employees would rather have?

3. do employees really understand the current benefits plan? How would they rank their benefits compared to those of other companies?

4. is the current benefit package a plus in recruiting and maintaining good employees?

5. is the company interested in containing and managing benefit costs?

6. does the company believe it is getting the most value for the dollars spent for benefits?

7. would the company be willing to commit to a thorough communications effort to inform employees about a new program?

8. is the company willing to explore new ground in the benefits area and be a leader among its competitors?

These and other questions should be examined by every organization making an effort to integrate management's objectives with employee needs and desires.

Flexible compensation programs are spreading fast. There are indicators that fifty percent of employers are either considering or in the process of implementing a flexible benefits plan. Indeed, a trend is in motion.

The changing demographics of the work force during the 1990's will require a more flexible strategy and approach to employee benefits if this form of compensation is to be meaningful to both employer and employee.

Strategy 9.8
Consider ESOPs and employee stock ownership.

Having some ownership in the enterprise for which one works is a compensation feature which fosters strong interest in the organization's success and growth, as well as commitment on the part of the worker to help it happen. Employee stock ownership plans (ESOP) were introduced to enable employees to acquire an equity interest in the employer organization, while at the same time providing them with a source of retirement income. As a compensation feature, ESOPs really have a double benefit. They provide a source of accumulating retirement funds with tax deferral advantages, and an opportunity to share in the company's growth and success.

From an employer's standpoint, there are also a number of positive aspects to ESOPs. These include tax incentives, improved employee moral, better employer-employee relations, and improved productivity.

There can, however, be negative perceptions of ESOPs including employees perhaps not wanting a substantial portion of their retirement income tied to the company's performance. ESOPs are complex and sometimes difficult for employees to understand and trust. ESOPs may not have the investment diversity of a qualified, defined contribution retirement plan.

Although ESOPs can provide compelling reasons for employees to remain with a company, an analysis of a number of factors should be conducted before a decision is made to implement such a plan.

1. What is the employer-employee relations climate?
2. What are the short and long range business prospects?
3. What is the impact on financial considerations such as; cash flow, earnings per share and the balance sheet?

In view of all the considerations it is extremely important that the company conduct a feasibility study before making the ESOP decision.

Chapter 10

People Growing Strategies

Good people want to grow professionally. They want to learn and practice new knowledge and skills. Through this process of what Abraham Maslow described as "self actualization", people enhance their personal value. At the same time, they are increasing their value to their employers.

It's important to enable these key people to grow at as rapid a pace as they wish. Don't worry about them leaving you as they become increasingly competent. If people feel they are still growing, and you give them the room to do so, they will stay with you.

Recognize that as people grow, they will desire even more opportunities to apply their talents and expertise to help your company and their careers. They will be looking for challenges, new challenges. Give them those opportunities; everyone benefits!

It's not smart to simply "throw" education and training at your people. The wise approach is to develop an individualized personal growth plan for each member of your team. Design the plan so that it is focused on achieving specific results that will support the employee's career, but keep it flexible as well.

Some designs will suggest a heavy orientation toward a college degree program of some sort. Others will lean in a different direction. The most effective will offer a variety of learning experiences to give the employee a well-rounded background. Consider both individual and group/team learning approaches, depending on your needs and desired results.

Designing an individualized plan with each employee enhances that person's feeling of importance--both self esteem and significance within the organization. These plans should be reduced to writing and reviewed on a periodic basis.

Strategy 10.1
Give people challenging responsibilities.

One way to enable people to grow is to give them increased responsibilities. Let them try new jobs. Allow them cross-training experiences to appreciate things from a variety of perspectives.

Recognize the expertise and experience of your people and find ways to tap that invaluable resource. When faced with a new job to be done, a challenging problem, or exciting opportunities opening up, invite input from your people. You would be amazed at what a little brainstorming can generate--even from people who are not directly connected with the particular issue under scrutiny.

What we're saying here is to encourage people to use their minds. Those wonderful folks working for you have some terrific ideas, even if they "just" operate a machine or do some mundane work each day. They see things differently and have grown from different roots.

One company was able to solve a problem because a custodian overheard a conversation and was brave enough to offer an objective perspective. The executives, who had gotten too close to the problem to see the obvious solution were flabbergasted, then highly appreciative. Every member of your team has something to offer.

Strategy 10.2
Support formal education.

Provide financial support to those employees interested in continuing their formal education. Their interest may be in a trade school, undergraduate college courses, or graduate courses at a university. While some employers limit their support to what they consider to be job-related courses, there are some other approaches to take.

You may want to offer a stronger degree of support for job-related courses than you do for courses that don't relate directly to the employee's work, but do contribute to a degree in the field. Be careful about being too narrow in your approach. While employees are learning about subjects that are not specifically job-related, they are also strengthening their self-discipline and self esteem.

When they complete the curriculum and graduate, they may suddenly become more marketable because they have the degree. Be wise and keep their loyalty by supporting the achievement of their career goals.

There are a number of different measures of how much support to give employees who take recognized courses. Some employers simply pay for the course up-front. The concern here is that the company may pay for courses and books without the student being able to complete the course for some reason. One way to balance the concerns is to give the employee a pay advance to cover tuition, fees, and books. When the course is completed satisfactorily, the repayment of the advance is waived.

Most will reimburse the employee upon completion of the course. Reimbursements are done in several ways. Sometimes the full amount of the student/employee's cost is covered, regardless of the level of achievement...as long as the course is completed. In other cases, the amount of the award is based on academic grade earned. Completion with an "A" would rate a 100% reimbursement. A "B" would earn 75%, a "C" 50%, and probably nothing below that level.

Some companies place a ceiling on the amount of money that will be disbursed per employee during any one semester or quarter. This helps control costs for the company and guides the employee to limit the course load. While encouraging growth, employers must be careful to help their employees understand they are employees first and company-supported students second.

Strategy 10.3
Offer learning materials for personal growth.

Establish and maintain a lending library of books, audiotapes, videotapes, and periodicals. These learning materials are available for the employee to borrow to continue personal and/or professional development.

Included in your library, which doesn't have to really be anything terribly formal, could be resource material on management styles and techniques, selling skills, and a wide range of technical topics. Books and tapes on personal skills such as listening, interpersonal relations, wellness, stress management, and time management are valuable to have.

Current periodicals, and even back issues, are valuable resource materials. Consider including local newspapers, business newspapers, and whatever trade publications and technical/professional journals apply to your field, adjacent fields, and/or your customer's fields of interest.

Some companies have extensive libraries, with the quantity of materials and the use strong enough to merit a full-time corporate librarian. You have to make the decision about what level of involvement and investment is best for your organization.

As young people enter and grow within your company, their mentors may want to spend some time in the library with them. These senior people can guide and encourage their proteges to read certain materials, absorb the knowledge from specific tapes, and follow applicable periodicals. Of course, by working with their proteges, the mentors themselves may find some things of interest to continue their own growth.

Strategy 10.4

Connect with outside resources for learning materials.

Encourage your people to borrow learning materials from community and university libraries. Inter-library networking makes the collections of a number of libraries easily accessible. Booksellers will often give discounts to people buying books or tapes for use in business.

Consider contacting booksellers located near your business location(s) to inquire about such discounts. They might be willing to extend discount privileges to any of your employees who present your company identification card. Such discounts could apply to any product purchased, not just business books specifically. This would not only be an employee benefit (at no cost to you), but would build more business for the bookseller. It's a win-win idea.

Strategy 10.5
Send people to outside seminars.

Your people can benefit greatly by participation in good quality seminars and workshops. The opportunities are boundless. These learning experiences, usually ranging from a half-day to a couple of days, are offered in central cities throughout the country. They are sponsored by commercial seminar companies, colleges and universities, and trade/professional associations.

Commercial Seminars

While some of these seminars, particularly a few of the commercial programs, pack people into a room and feed them with a volume of information, many of the opportunities available are quite valuable. Look for those that will have a relatively low attendance, so your people will have a chance to interact with the instructor and fellow participants.

Even those that simply load participants with information are helpful, especially if a number of people from the same company attend. If you only send one or a few people, require the attendees to share their new knowledge with others when they come back to work. (*See Strategy 10.6*) This sharing not only inspires people to pay closer attention in the session, it reinforces the learning and enables others to share the experience vicariously. Emphasis should be placed on how the knowledge gained applies in *your* work setting.

The commercial seminar companies do a fairly good job of blanketing the countryside with promotional literature. In fact, you may find that your organization receives multiple copies of the same brochures. These companies use various sources to build their mailing lists, so your postal carrier will be bringing you all sorts of goodies.

It's tempting to simply toss the brochures into the trash without even looking at them. Take a moment, even if you don't plan to send anyone, and look at what's being taught. The topic and the outline may give you some insight into trends and suggest some topics you should address in internal training sessions. Some of the national commercial companies will send trainers into your company for in-house presentations, if that would be more economical for you.

School-Sponsored Programs

Colleges and universities throughout the country offer both credit and non-credit educational programs that can help your people grow. Consider both kinds of opportunities in guiding the development of your employees.

The credit course alternative is discussed in detail in Strategy 10.2, so we won't spend much time on it here. We do want to encourage you, if you have sufficient people and scheduling control, to consider offering credit college courses on your company's premises. Many colleges will send instructors to you, making it convenient for your employees and offering opportunities for focused discussion regarding situations in *your* company. You'll have built-in, practical, meaningful case studies.

Non-credit courses are offered by the continuing education departments of hundreds of universities and colleges. To learn what is being done in your vicinity, call the schools that serve your area. The schools are not as aggressive in their marketing, as a rule, as the commercial seminar companies, although you may receive some brochures from time to time. You'll be more effective seeking the information of your own volition.

Non-credit programs range from half-day sessions to multi-week courses. Topics include both "hard" and "soft" subjects, from relaxation methods to high technology or very technical classes. Sometimes these programs can also be brought in-house. They are taught by university instructors in some instances, but even more often by contract instructors with expertise in a particular topic. Quality will vary considerably, so don't hesitate to ask for outlines and references.

Many high schools offer programs for adults. The greatest effort in this area comes from vocationally-oriented high schools, but there are many opportunities. Again, you have to take the initiative in most cases to discover what is offered. Some of these schools have outreach programs where they will send instructors into your company.

Trade and Professional Associations

An increasing number of trade and professional organizations are offering learning opportunities for members. The majority of these sessions are provided as part of the program at conventions or conferences, but some associations have established education departments to help meet member needs outside the convention environment.

Check to see whether your trade association is one of those offering seminars, workshops, or courses in various cities around the country. The programs range from retreats for senior executives to seminars and workshops for managers at all levels to skills training and technical updates for hourly employees.

Some associations present mini-seminars at their conventions to see which ones attract the most member interest. Those topics are then offered as one- or two-day seminars in central locations for member companies. If this sort of service is not available from your industry association, they might welcome your expression of interest and suggestions for topics to be addressed.

Many professions, particularly those with licensing requirements in various states, offer association-managed certification programs. Members must meet certain qualifications, usually including educational and time-in-service components, to earn the initial certification. Sometimes the educational opportunities are provided by the association or society; sometimes the member must submit validation of having met the requirements through alternative sources meeting sponsor-established criteria.

To maintain their certification, members holding the credential must show evidence of their continuing educational development by investing a minimum number of hours in courses, seminars, or workshops during each ensuing one-year or multi-year period.

Even if the membership organization does not provide the actual learning opportunities, the certification programs may provide a structured design of recommended education and training to offer in-house. This will at least offer a course to follow in working with employees to support their professional development.

Strategy 10.6
Have learners pass their training along to others.

As your people participate in various learning experiences, under the sponsorships described in the previous section, encourage them to share the knowledge they learned with other members of your team. You'll find that, while not every topic lends itself to this kind of pass-along, quite a few will.

The method of sharing will depend on the people involved, the nature of the material, and your company's facilities. Don't try to make every opportunity fit any kind of a mold. Some knowledge will be best shared on a one-to-one personal basis; other information will be communicated more effectively in a seminar or lecture mode.

When your company is paying for an employee's training outside the organization, establish the expectation that a condition of payment is that the knowledge gained be shared with others. Don't expect your employee to present a seminar verbatim. Most seminar participants don't have the combination of knowledge and presentation skills that professional seminar leaders do.

Instead, invite the employee to share highlights or key points with his/her manager and others who might benefit. As much as reasonable, let the means for communicating this knowledge be determined by the employee. Some people are *terrified* of standing up to give a speech. Don't force people into doing things that aren't comfortable for them.

To assure worthwhile transfer of the material learned, give the employee the time and space needed. An extended lunch hour, a conference room, a chalkboard or flip chart, or other support will enable the employee to communicate effectively.

When learners know that the knowledge shared in seminars or workshops will have to be taught to others upon returning to work, they pay more attention and absorb more in sessions they attend. Everyone benefits more when the learning is made a part of the job, rather than just something extra that is done without relation to achieving better results in the work environment.

Strategy 10.7
Help people grow into bigger jobs.

While the Peter Principle (postulated by Dr. Laurence J. Peter) suggests that people can be promoted to their level of incompetence, I assert that many people are held back from achieving their full potential.

In too many organizations, people in management and supervisory positions invest an inordinate amount of time protecting their own position. This effort includes guarding secrets such as details of particular projects, puffing-up one's own importance, and holding back subordinates from professional growth.

These misguided folks think that if one of their people becomes too good, he or she might be promoted...even perhaps beyond his/her boss's position. This would certainly not look good, the protective bosses muse.

Actually, quite the contrary is true. One of the measures of a boss's effectiveness is how well the subordinates perform. If they are trained and developed well, they will be able to do their jobs more competently. They will also be more prepared to take on other assignments and other opportunities in the organization.

As these people move into positions where they can accept--and perform--new challenges, the boss becomes known and appreciated as a people-builder. Those kinds of bosses are most valuable, because they have proven ability to teach and empower people to grow. As the bosses move into more responsible positions, co-workers will be confident of their ability to develop a productive team in practically any situation.

Many supervisors and lower level managers dampen their own opportunities for advancement because they have not developed their people to be able to take their place. If you want to be promoted, train one or more people to succeed you.

As you prepare your people for jobs with a wider scope, more responsibility, or a higher position in the company, their enhanced capacity will enable them to perform better as a member of your team. You can derive both short-term and long-term benefits by investing your time, interest, energy, and other resources in growing your people.

Your good people's appreciation of your interest and support, will inspire them to stay with you as loyal members of your team.

Strategy 10.8

Enable people to discover the wealth of talents they have.

Each of us is capable of doing quite a bit. We have, over the years, developed a wide range of talents, abilities, expertise, experiences, and aptitudes. All this capacity adds up to a tremendous amount of potential.

How much do you know about the real potential of your people, let alone yourself? If you're like most of us, you are so busy with the many challenges of getting things done and leading people toward high achievement, there is a tendency not to look deeply enough.

Some of your better people are involved, or have been, in activities that helped them discover, develop, and practice new skills and talents. While some of this may have been on the job, a significant portion of personal and professional development takes place in non-work settings.

Are your people involved in community activities such as Scouting, Little League, church groups, civic clubs, or fraternal organizations? Are they in leadership positions or other positions of responsibility? Does the experience they gain in those activities strengthen their capacity to perform for you and your organization? Would the skills and background they have gained make them eligible for a different kind of work and/or a leadership position on-the- job?

Quite often, people active in their community develop a high potential for leadership and accomplishment they are not able to apply at work. They put in their time on-the-job, eager for the end of the work day so they can return to the fulfilling work they really enjoy. Their focus is gradually more on their non-work activity. Result: they become less loyal to their employer and more apt to leave to accept a position where their talents are appreciated and useful.

I personally experienced this phenomenon early in my career. My work assignments were nowhere near as exciting, challenging, and rewarding as the higher level of involvement I had in civic activities. After a frustrating 18 months, I resigned my position in an executive development program with a Fortune 500 company to accept a turn-around opportunity with a much smaller employer. I might still be with the major corporation today if that company's managers had recognized what I had to offer.

There are countless ways for people to learn new skills, strengthen old ones, and practice and polish their abilities in the work environment. Give your employees special assignments, cross-training and experience, and other opportunities to gain new knowledge and capacities. Enable them to experiment, to get their feet wet with something new.

Not everything your people try will be successful. Some of us have mechanical aptitude, some have fine abilities to reason and think logically, others are great organizers or smooth persuaders. Testing your people's capacity, in non-threatening situations, will give them--and you--a chance to discover and apply their talents in satisfying ways.

The enhanced level of self-worth, enmeshed with their work accomplishment and development, will build people's confidence and loyalty. Their personal growth will be part and parcel of their work with you.

Strategy 10.9
Encourage intellectual growth.

Much of the training and development being offered in corporate America is directed toward technical skill building, management and leadership, sales and marketing, customer service, application of technology, and personal growth topics such as time management, coping with stress, decision making, and dress for success.

Few of these topics inspire learners to stretch intellectually. Your good people could benefit from growth opportunities to learn to think more clearly and rationally. Experiential courses in logic or creativity might strengthen your organization's problem-solving capacity.

The **THINK** sign has become commonplace in the workplace, but we still encounter numerous difficulties because people just don't think. Television programming, fast food restaurants, quick-read shallow-coverage periodicals, and other trends in our lives have made it possible to survive quite nicely without thinking very deeply. Leading edge employers will find ways to help people reason better.

Organizations striving to gain the strongest possible return on their investment in human resources are creating opportunities for people to talk with each other. They are discovering that their good people have a considerable amount to share with each other, that they have quite a bit of power in their own ranks.

Usually, everyone is so busy accomplishing the work of the day, no one has time (or takes time) just to sit and talk. When a piece of time is set aside for people to discuss issues and concerns, especially with the help of a professional facilitator, an incredible amount of growth and progress occurs. It's amazing what can happen during a retreat. We've seen significant results with our clients in only a day or two, even before constructive follow-up.

There is a real need for people to learn and practice the basic skills of thinking and cooperating. A surprising number of people are actually afraid to think for themselves. It's a threatening trend that must be overcome if people are to function to their full potential. Interestingly, we've responded to specific requests from some of our clients by providing workshops on Common Sense!

Strategy 10.10
Assign special projects.

To give your people opportunities to broaden their knowledge, perspectives, and experiences, offer them special projects that are beyond their comfort zone. These should not be "make work" assignments, but legitimate work that will contribute to the forward movement of the organization.

Furnish the resources, including time, for the appropriate devotion to meeting the challenge. Provide access to needed data, people, and expertise so your shining stars can learn, grow, and achieve.

The assignments do not have to be earth-shaking projects that will change the direction of the organization's progress, although some of your people might benefit from such a study. One of our clients asked middle managers to assess whether the company should remain in several facilities, consolidate into the existing plant, or move everything to an entirely new building. Those involved learned quite a bit about the corporate world beyond their functional areas.

An increasing number of companies take hourly production line employees along to industry trade shows. The selected employees learn about the latest technology, what other companies are doing, how buying decisions are made, and how various components of the industry relate to each other. They return to work with a whole new perspective. In some cases, the employees who make the trip are expected to share their new knowledge with their co-workers. (*See Strategy 10.6.*)

For other ideas, how about having machine operators gain some experience in set-up? Your customer service people might benefit from going along on some sales calls, then critiquing the process. Have you sent production supervisors or quality control people on visits to your customers' sites?

How many of your retail employees have shopped the competition and reported on their findings?

Be creative! Get people involved in new product design, market studies, public relations events, and industry associations. Expand their vision, then watch that new insight and energy go to work for you, the employee, and the organization! It's a win-win-win situation.

Strategy 10.11
Build competency deliberately.

A growing number of companies are beginning to do career planning with their employees, especially the people identified as the rising stars. It's a valuable practice to engage in with all your people.

As you identify the competencies needed for each person to move ahead in his/her career, start making a list. Measure the employee's current capability against what will be required for future opportunities with the organization. Prioritize the needs as you both see them. When will they be needed: a month, a year, three years from now?

From this list, develop a plan to enable the team member to expand his/her professional capacity through a deliberate, organized plan of competency-building. Indicate who will be responsible for each component of the plan. Will the employee be expected to take a course or gain some specific skill? Will the supervisor make training or experience available? Will arrangements be made jointly, with the supervisor and subordinate learning together?

What resources will be needed to implement the plan? Personal or paid time for the employee to learn? Funds to pay for training programs or college courses? Time off from normal duties for growth experiences?

After you have established a realistic timetable, initiate the development process. Meet with the employee periodically to review progress and make any needed adjustments in the plan. Maintain a written record in the employee's personnel folder for permanency.

As your people advance themselves, be sure to recognize their achievement. Letters of congratulations or praise from superiors, public announcements in house organs or even in local newspapers, and interim promotions or special assignments (*See Strategy 10.10*) are alternative methods to mark growth.

Strategy 10.12
Provide incentives for growth.

If you encourage and enable your people to learn and grow without some sort of payoff, you may encounter a couple of risks.

One risk is that the employees may become disillusioned. They are hoping for promotions, opportunities to put their new knowledge into practice, or at least some enhanced status in the organization. If those avenues are closed to them, they may lose their enthusiasm for personal growth.

Another risk is that you may help people grow professionally to become fine, highly productive employees for someone else. Be prepared to utilize the new knowledge and skills your people will gain. Help them put their new strength to use in viable efforts in your organization. Make the whole experience, learning and application, meaningful.

Yes, it is worthy to learn merely for the sake of learning. However, the judicious use of corporate funds suggests that monies invested in employee development should have a positive return to the company. Your people feel the same way: the investment of their time and energy should reap a reward.

As much as possible, establish your criteria for response to employee growth in advance. Clarify what you expect from the employee, and what the employee can expect from you. Unless extenuating circumstances make it impossible, fulfill your part of the bargain. If you fail to keep your promises, especially without an explanation to the employee, you will lose credibility. And you may lose a valued employee.

Follow through to achieve the maximum benefit for all concerned.

SECTION THREE

Chapter 11

Tactics for Implementing Strategies

In the pages preceding this chapter, we have discussed over 125 different strategies for keeping good people. We have seen how doing things to keep good people will also keep them productive. Being productive encourages people to want to stay on the job. It's a win-win cycle.

In a planning scheme, the strategies are the approaches you take to gain an advantage. Tactics are the means by which you apply the strategies to accomplish your objectives.

Each of the strategies can stand alone. Each can be applied to make a positive difference in your organization. The strategies can be applied by managers at any level, in any kind of functional position.

When the strategy is applied, there will be an impact at all levels beneath the manager who implements it. In some cases, the effect will be direct and immediate. In other cases, it may

235

be less direct and less immediate, depending on a variety of circumstances.

The quickest, and most apparent results will be seen among the manager's direct reports. If nothing else is done by any other members of the management team, the impact will diminish as the implementation of the strategy moves down through the chain of command. The influence on the way the organization does business will depend on how far the implementing manager is from the front line, where the action is.

There are three ways to enhance the effect of the manager's efforts:

1. involve subordinate managers in a vertical implementation
2. involve peer managers in a cooperative implementation
3. involve higher level managers to increase the strength of the intervention.

Vertical Implementation

Making the strategies work requires concentrated, consistent effort by the implementing manager(s). The further down, and up, the chain of command you go, the more potential you have to get the results you seek.

If you are a first line manager with direct responsibility for hourly workers or salaried employees on the firing line, you have a considerable amount of influence over the attitudes and behavior of your people. Your team is comprised of the people who are the hands-on, get-the-job-done, folks who accomplish the real work of the organization.

In many companies, these front-line employees are highly sensitive to meeting the demands of the customer as well as fulfilling your expectations. Whether in a retail or service environment, in distribution, in manufacturing, or in research and development, their focus is on doing what the customer needs and wants.

These people are usually among the most valuable in an organization, although sometimes senior management acts as though this is not the case. The application of the strategies is important with these folks to keep them happy, productive, and loyal. What they do--or don't do, how they perform, and the attitudes they display, directly affect customer satisfaction.

Because of their limited exposure to more senior members of your organization, front line employees have an especially strong relationship with their supervisor. Over time, it becomes a sort of bond. To the employee, his/her supervisor *is* the company.

If the first line supervisor performs well, implementing the strategies in a deliberate and organized fashion, members of the front line team will probably feel satisfied, valuable, and productive. There will be less chance of them leaving to accept other positions. They will feel a part of the company and will probably remain in their position of comfort.

If the first line supervisor does not perform well, does not implement the strategies well, there will be friction between management and labor. Workers will transfer their feelings about their supervisor to the company as a whole, building a dangerous animosity. Productivity will drop, and so will feelings of loyalty.

After a period of time working for a supervisor who is not focused on keeping good people, employees become restless and dissatisfied, ready to jump ship at the slightest provocation. Their attitudes of disloyalty and irritation can be highly contagious, poisoning even those who had been outstanding employees prior to the development of negative feelings. They will seek out others with similar opinions, eventually blowing the difficulties out of proportion.

When you have this kind of a situation, and it may have already developed in your organization, you have to apply the strategies with a higher level of intensity and dedication. Plan your actions more carefully to gradually get results.

As was brought out in Strategy 6.23, when you have a difficult situation, your best solution may be to terminate the employment of the "infected" people. This is always difficult to do, especially if some of the people had been good performers in the past. The longer you wait, the more difficult it becomes...and the higher the risk of further damage. To hold your good people, sometimes you have to remove the bad surgically.

Be alert for the "bad apple" in your organization. There are those people out there, as we all know, who are negative and/or won't go along with the program. This is not to say you want everyone to conform and march like toy soldiers. Nonconforming is healthy in organizations. That's what inspires innovation and leadership. Just be sure the nonconformity is directed in positive ways, and not into activities that could have a negative impact.

If the implementing manager is at a higher level, more removed from the day-to-day action, the impact of strategic intervention on the front line will not be as strong. To achieve the desired results, the higher level manager must work vertically. Working down through the chain of command, the leader must persuade each lower level manager to support efforts to implement the strategies successfully.

If there is a missing link anywhere in the chain, the process will not have the maximum effect. In fact, if there is resistance or even just apathy on the part of any manager in the vertical chain, the results could be negative.

I observed this recently in a company where a senior level manager demonstrated the approach described in this book. The first line managers felt the same way he did, and liked what he was saying, but were virtually powerless because the middle managers didn't support the process. They were more concerned with protecting their own positions. In reality, the first line managers were disenfranchised in their efforts to turn the company around and make a significant positive difference.

The implementation of the strategies works best if the implementing manager, at any level, has the commitment and support of his/her superior *and* subordinate managers.

Managers without support from their superiors feel practically powerless in the implementation of many of the strategies. Subordinate team members need to feel that their leader has the support of the next higher level, or the words sound empty. Without having that support from above, some managers are afraid to attempt even a small strategic effort for fear of being caught out on a limb. Others just opt out and do nothing.

This need for support goes all the way up the organization. It's not just at the operational level.

Good, worthwhile results can be seen from unilateral implementation of the strategies, but the power just isn't there. Managers at any level should apply the strategies as best they can, but everyone has to be involved to really make it work.

Powers of persuasion work well going up the organization ladder, not just down. The more successful you are in gaining the visible, involved support of your superior and subordinate managers, the more chance you will have of making a difference as an implementing manager.

Cooperative Implementation

A department manager, or a vertical chain of managers in a particular functional area, can make a difference. Most organizations of any size will have a number of managers at each level. Cooperation is needed among these people.

To make your efforts to keep good people, and keep them productive throughout the company, your policies and their strategic implementation have to be as consistent as possible. You'll have some differences because of differences in personalities and styles of managers. The more consistent you are, the greater will be your results.

Your objective is to help the managers, in all areas of the organization, to speak with one voice. If profanity is frowned on in one part of the company and not another, for example, the "mixed signals" get confusing. People aren't sure just what the company wants.

With widely varying approaches, you may also generate a overt or unconscious competition between supervisors. Sometimes this is healthy; often it becomes counterproductive, especially for the manager whose people want to transfer out to another department.

Teams of managers at each level should meet regularly to examine how they are working with their people. What "messages" are they sending by their actions, by their application of the various strategies. How are the various functions of the company working together, or not, and how can implementation of some of the strategies make a difference?

The cooperative process will be more difficult to initiate in some companies than in others. Your ease of cooperation will depend on past practices, experiences of the managers, and the way senior management handles the situation.

One way to start is simply to have a meeting of all the managers you want to cooperate. Explain the concept and your expectations. Emphasize that these people are a key team in building and maintaining the organization's strength...and in keeping good people. Be open to questions, resistance, and skepticism.

Introduce this book to them. It would be valuable for each member of the management team to have a personal copy of *Keeping Good People* for personal study and reference. Encourage them to underline, make marginal notes, and discuss strategies with each other and with you.

In subsequent meetings, discuss particular strategies you want to implement across departmental lines. Talk about how the application of the strategy might affect each manager and that manager's team. Strive for consensus--about the value of the strategy, the commitment to implementation, and the way it will be done. Remember consistency.

During this introductory phase, in particular, it would probably be wise to use the services of professional trainers to build a sense of "teamness" and to sharpen management and leadership skills. Not surprisingly, most people in management positions, at all levels, are sadly deficient in the skills and knowledge needed to do their jobs properly. In some industries there has been an increasing emphasis on management training and development, but we still have a long way to go.

Professional trainers and consultants, especially outsiders who have not been a part of the organization, can also serve you as facilitators of discussion in your management meetings. Often, participants in such gatherings will say little. They don't "buy in" to the program, producing those counterproductive weak links.

You need to get everyone involved, bringing out ideas, feelings, perspectives, and reactions. The sharpened skills of experienced facilitators enable them to build the involvement and the interchange that could significantly increase your chances for success.

If you do use an outside facilitator, that person's role is to stimulate the discussion and decision making of your people. The role is *not* to determine your policy or to "force" people to go along with something even if they're not comfortable with it.

Your leadership role should be responsive to, and interactive with, your facilitator. The outside professional is there strictly to help you do your job better, not to do your job for you.

Consider your people, your organization, and take the steps necessary to build commitment and consistency among peer groups of managers. As they collaborate more, you'll see positive changes among each of their work teams and in the operation as a whole.

Involve Higher Level Managers

It should come as no big surprise that the higher you go in the organization, the greater power and impact the manager has on the behavior of people and the direction of the overall team.

To keep good people, and keep them highly productive, the leadership needs to come from as high in the organization as possible. The higher the source of commitment, the greater will be the results.

Ideally, the chief executive officer of the company will assume an active leadership role in the confirmation and implementation of the strategies. Even if the senior person sees the strategies as "of course we should do that here," subordinate managers may not hear (or accept) the message.

You can't assume that "everyone does it" in leadership today. Too many people set their own direction or just float waiting for the next pronouncement from On High. To build consistent implementation of these strategies, to really have the kind of organization-wide impact that builds corporate reputations, top management must be involved.

The involvement can not be mere lip service. Saying, "I think this stuff is all on-target, so go do it," won't work. People are looking for an active commitment. They want to see you actually practicing the strategies...and supporting those subordinate managers who do the same.

I remember my frustration talking with the president of a manufacturing company a number of years ago. I was trying to emphasize the critical importance of using outside professional trainers and facilitators in his company. He didn't think he needed help. He viewed consultants with disdain, figuring he had all the answers.

This company president bought copies of *In Search Of Excellence*, the stimulating book by Tom Peters and Bob

Waterman. He gave the book to all his managers on a Thursday morning, asking them to read it over the weekend. "We're going to start doing this Monday morning!", he exclaimed.

The managers read the book with enthusiasm and came in Monday fired-up and ready to excel. The president praised them and encouraged them to go forth and do something. However, he explained that he was pretty busy, would have to stay in his office to get his work done, and would not be able to join them.

About a year later, the company went belly-up. The bankruptcy put them out of business and put several hundred people out of work.

What happened, obviously, is that the bankruptcy began in the president's office. Remember that your people need active and visible leadership. You can't influence people vicariously. Leadership is shared, not delegated or assigned. Try to have someone lead in your stead and you are abdicating your position.

The more the organization's leaders work together as a team, speaking with a single voice that is backed up by consistent action, the better your results will be. You'll have a more productive workforce with greater stability, satisfaction, and pride.

You'll be on the exciting cutting edge. You'll have the power to excel.

Chapter 12

Combining Strategic Approaches for Optimum Results

The format of this book has presented strategies in individual and, for the most part, independent sections. This design was used to call attention to each strategy as an approach unto itself and to make the book more readable and usable as a reference work.

As you implement the strategies, it is important to appreciate the interdependence of these techniques. While many of the strategies can be tactically implemented as tools by themselves, they become most effective when related to other strategies.

In fact, many of the strategies depend on other strategies being in place or being implemented concurrently. There are close linkages connecting the kinds of strategies we've discussed. It is advised that you read through all the strategies before trying to work with any of them to any great degree. Gain an appreciation for the *comprehensive* approach.

In leading people, and inspiring them to stay with you, it is helpful to appreciate the complexity of their environment, especially from your people's perspective. If you concentrate on making one aspect better, while ignoring a related aspect, you may get results that are different from what you expect.

Management gurus and evangelists urge corporate leaders to leap into making changes in structure, policy, procedures, and people. Some of these self-styled experts exhort managers with rash pronouncements like, "Don't just stand there, do something!"

I encourage you to take a different approach: *"Don't Just Do Something, Stand There."* Look before you leap. What is it that you are trying to accomplish? What strategic approaches will enable you to achieve your objectives? How can they best be implemented? By whom? When, and how quickly? What resources and support will be needed? What are the implications of what we are about to do?

Strengthening one area of your operation may weaken another. Or, your efforts may point out weak areas that you had not been that sensitive to previously. You may become aware of some vulnerabilities that you hadn't seen before.

As you deliberately apply the strategies for keeping good people, consider *all* the aspects of your organization. Try to anticipate the reaction/response of your people as you formally introduce a strategy and strive to make it work. Even when you try to gradually slip into enhancing a strategic approach, your people will have a pretty good idea what you are doing.

Don't try to sneak in with these strategies. They should be applied overtly, deliberately, with the full knowledge and solicited cooperation of everyone involved. Your efforts will be appreciated by your good people, and they will support your efforts. This support may be longer in coming than you would prefer, based on past history and present circumstances.

A number of the strategies presented in *Keeping Good People* may already be in place in your organization. Even if you believe they are part of the way you and your people do business, you should confirm the belief for yourself. Quite often, managers (especially senior managers) honestly believe that their people have certain understandings that they simply do not have.

To confirm for yourself, talk with and listen carefully to your subordinate managers and their people. Ask open-ended questions that will put them in the position of telling you what they think, what they believe, what they do. Comparing that input against your desired situation will give you a more realistic idea of what strategies people perceive.

Once you understand the reality of your situation, you can plan the tactics you will follow to integrate the strategies into your organization. Build on the strengths you already have, gradually folding in commitment to the new strategies.

Note, please, my use of the word, *gradually*. Changes will not come as quickly as you might like or expect. The old habits have taken a long time to become part of your people, part of your culture. They won't just, *poof*, change overnight. Be happy to make a little progress each day, but strive for conscious improvement each day.

Make your improvements conscious in your own mind, and also in the minds of your direct reports and their people. Keep awareness high that you expect people to excel, that you expect the organization to excel.

As you implement the strategies, you will probably discover that some of them are compatible. When you have the opportunity, implement companion strategies together. One may well support another.

For example, Strategy 6.16 talks about promoting a healthy working environment. As you implement parts of Strategy 6.45 to maintain the best atmospheric conditions, you'll support a healthy working environment. Reducing stress, Strategy 7.30, might also fit right in. Some sort of a wellness program might be a sensible answer for you. Using Strategy 10.10, you may assign development of a program to one or more people (a task force?) to give them some valuable research and organization experience.

Talk with members of your management team to learn their perspectives of the various strategies and how they "fit" in your organization. Discuss where you are falling short, in lip service or follow-through, to see how you can improve individually and as a team.

Some of your fellow managers might be somewhat skittish about applying these strategies. People like to stay in their comfort zones, and using these strategies consistently and continually will create some discomfort. Relate what you are trying to do in terms these other people can understand and deal with. Meet people where they are; know their positions. Then, gradually, move them toward your position...where you would like them to be.

Force yourself, and your colleagues, to always look at your people and your organization as a *system*. Everything is inter-related.

Chapter 13

Focus on Each Individual's Needs

Your organization is comprised of individuals. A variety of individuals. Each person striving for his/her own goals...in work and in life. To gain the most from your people, and to inspire them to remain part of your team, it is vital that you recognize them as individuals.

As long as being a part of your organization fills the needs and is compatible with an employee's values, that employee will probably stay with you. Most people seek what we might describe as a "comfort zone" in their careers, where they can feel challenged, useful, productive, empowered, and appreciated. When they find a job that has such a comfort zone, they usually settle in for an indefinite period of time.

If the job does not include a complete comfort zone, if all needs and values are not met, the employee will be restless. The degree of restlessness varies from individual to individual, based on the importance placed on unmet aspects of the desired comfort zone.

The key, then, is to learn all you can about what motivates each individual member of your team. What are each person's personal career goals? How well can your group respond to the fulfillment of those goals, now and into the future?

What kinds of challenges does your rising star want in the working environment? Are the desired challenges more of a project nature, or does this individual want the challenge of the increased responsibility that comes with assuming new positions of leadership? Is the interest more in narrow, task-focused challenges, or in wider position-focused arenas?

How fast does the individual want to move along the career path? Is this person a fast climber or a steady-as-you-go type? Should the path be fairly well chartered early in the employment relationship, or would this rising star prefer a less structured reactive arrangement in which career moves are determined by emerging opportunities?

Job Satisfaction

We use "job satisfaction" as an all-encompassing term to describe how people feel about their positions of employment. A number of factors enter into the measurement of job satisfaction, most of which we've already talked about in this book.

Our concern at this stage must be to investigate and analyze the job satisfaction level of each individual. What factors define job satisfaction, and how does the individual measure them? It does not matter how you measure them; the concern is with how each employee gauges his or her own personal level of job satisfaction.

The level of job satisfaction significantly influences an employee's stability with a particular employer. The roots are very shallow if the job satisfaction level is low. They go deeper as the level increases. Setbacks are always possible; it's a fragile, volatile equilibrium that must be monitored and maintained.

If satisfaction with most aspects of a job is high, an employee may tend to overlook the areas that aren't as high as desired. The positive can offset the negative. If the balance starts going the other way, the negative aspects take on a new significance and the process of disequilibrium can occur very quickly.

Attention must be given, therefore, to discovering what weights the employee places on various parts of the personal job satisfaction equation. Then, take concrete steps to meet as many of those elements as possible, as *well* as possible.

Be careful you don't go overboard meeting the needs of any one employee, particularly if your support might be at the expense of others. If you don't maintain your focus on the big picture, you could easily invest more in keeping one employee happy than it is worth to keep that employee. Hard as it is to accept, especially when you are in the emotional middle of a campaign to hold an employee, everyone is expendable.

Useful, Productive

Today's employee wants to feel useful. Each individual member of your team wants to feel a high level of productivity, that results are being achieved because of the personal effort.

In every way that you can, help your people see exactly what they are contributing to the accomplishment of the organization's mission. There will be a contribution, of course, because without any contribution to desired ends we would have no reason to have those people on the team. Most employees simply don't ever see what kind of a contribution they really do make. When is the last time you talked with your direct reports, those who report directly to you, about their personal contributions to your team effort?

People know when they are productive. They also know when they are not. Part of this judgment is measurable; part of it is a feeling that people have about their real value to their employer. No one really wants to be a parasite on society, when the opportunity is there to earn one's own way.

Some of the jobs to be done in your organization might involve people waiting for what seems to be a long time for the next piece of work to be done. That's just the way the system works. Appreciate that the waiting time may become agonizing, especially when others around you are productively occupied. With your sensitivity, help that person accept the waiting gracefully without losing esteem.

I remember earning part of my way through school at Hiram College setting up and serving banquets. There was a period in our work, after everything was set and we weren't needed for a little while. I felt that I should be doing something, other than sitting, to earn my pay during those long stand-by moments. My supervisor and mentor told me something I have never forgotten: "they also serve who only sit and wait." Help your people put things in perspective, so they'll always feel that they are serving.

Empowerment

The concept of employee empowerment is relatively new, at least in its definition and conscious position in the workplace. It's not revolutionary; there are employers who have been empowering their people for years. Empowerment is a vital aspect of today's working environment and is unquestionably important in your efforts to keep many of your good people.

Historically, during the 20th century we have spent most of our management time directing the efforts of others. That's what managers have been expected to do: tell others what to do. In carrot-and-stick fashion, if people did well what they were told to do, they were rewarded with better jobs, more money, more authority over others. If they didn't perform, they were punished with discipline, lower incomes, dead-end jobs, and diminished social status.

Moving away from telling everyone what to do, how to do it, and when to do it, we began to emphasize enabling people to do things in the workplace. Providing varying levels of support, we gave up some of the managerial control over everything employees did. The techniques of definitive reward and punishment were replaced by less obvious approaches of motivational management. The concept of leadership wrestled with the concept of management in an often uncomfortable effort to make a transition.

Empowerment takes enabling a quantum leap down the road of making employees responsible and accountable for their own performance. This is accomplished by giving people more control over the way things are done and over the resources needed. More and more, employees are also determining what should be done, and in what order of priority.

The message heard by empowered employees is that everything is in their hands. They have the power to do things their way, but with an even higher expectation that the objectives will be met. Much of the reward and punishment motivation from the autocratic approach now becomes intrinsic.

People want to be empowered, both as employees and personally in other aspects of their lives. This becomes critically important in an age where people feel practically powerless to influence the events in the world around them. At the same time, the idea of having so much power over one's own destiny is intimidating for some people. They just aren't ready to handle it.

Appreciation

Each individual wants to be appreciated. Each person seeks that appreciation in a different form. Some merely want an affirmation, others want you to bring on the brass bands and the parade. Some folks prefer a quiet recognition, a one-on-one personal communication from a supervisor or some other significant person(s). There are those on the other extreme who want "the whole world" to know you appreciate what they do. And, of course, there are many variations in the middle of that continuum.

For maximum effectiveness, tailor your expression of appreciation to each individual employee. Learn enough about them that you can understand their preferences, then meet those personal expectations.

The two important points are that you must show appreciation for work done, for knowledge gained, for skills applied, for attitudes shown. But, you must show that appreciation in ways that are wholly appropriate for the individual with whom you are dealing.

If you neglect to show appreciation, or if you express your feelings in ways that are not befitting to the individual or to the situation, the negative response will be the same. Your actions must be genuine. They must be sincere. If they are not, your efforts to praise or reward someone may backfire. Always be appropriate for the specific individual in question.

You can't win 'em all

No matter how hard you try, you will not be able to keep all your good people. There are various reasons for this, some of which are completely out of your control. Put things in perspective and know that some people you would like to keep are going to leave.

There are several reasons for their departures. One is some sort of dissatisfaction with the kind of work assigned. Another reason relates to the way work is done in your organization. Some folks will leave because of their fellow employees. Others won't see the opportunities they seek working with you, and you may not be able to offer them what they want.

Still other people move on just because it's time to move on. There are those who don't want to work for any one organization for too long. Any organization. It's nothing against you, personally, or against the employing organization. It's just an inner drive to keep moving, to keep growing, to keep trying out new experiences.

Many of the people in today's workforce, and many of those entering the workforce in the 1990s, are restless by nature. Part of their value system tells them not to stay in one place for very long. "Gain some experience, then move on" is the message they hear from their inner voice. They tend not to put down roots in any aspect of their lives, acting almost like modern-day nomads.

In researching this book, I talked with some of these people who were perfectly satisfied with their jobs. Their employer could do nothing more to satisfy them any further. They just needed to move on. There are new things to see and do, new horizons to be seen, new dragons to be met and conquered.

When it's time for people to leave, wish them good luck and get out of their way. Begging on bended knee for someone to stay with you is not becoming, is viewed with disdain by other employees, and will cloud your thinking as you search for the right person to succeed your departing star.

Know that, even though you might give them the world and promise them more, some people will leave anyway. As my friend and colleague, Joe Charbonneau, is fond of saying, "of all the people who will never leave me, I'm the only one." Be true unto yourself, and everything else will work out.

You can't keep all your good people. Don't expect to. Not only are you training and preparing them for greater opportunities, they themselves are seeking new horizons for themselves. As a balanced, mission-focused employer, you can not be all things to all employees.

You contribute to the development of people. Some will stay, some will go. All of them will give you something back. Enjoy those "somethings" you receive, and pass them along to the new people eager to join your team.

Enjoy working with all those wonderful individuals who comprise your unique team. Help them become more of what they are, and what they want to be.

Chapter 14

A Perspective on the Future

Some folks say it is impossible to predict the future. Others argue that the past is prologue. Historians caution that those who do not study the past are doomed to repeat it. Economists tell us that everything moves in cycles. Seers suggest that the future is now. Futurists talk in terms of trends.

Well, considering all that, I suppose we really can't predict the future with certainty. Nothing is definite. We can join the futurists and study the trends, while we accept input from the historians about what will form the foundation for the fate that awaits us.

Based on today, and our recent past, we can predict with a fair degree of assurance, our immediate future. Ten years, a decade, seems like a long time. Especially when the end of that period will roll us over into the next century. January 1,

2000, seems almost forbidding; yet it will be another day just like tomorrow.

People

Considering what we can predict for the historical decade of the 1990s, it is obvious that people will continue to be the most vital resource for practically every kind of organization that produces goods or services. Some jobs will remain pretty much the same as they have been, but others will change dramatically with the gradual introduction of new technology in the workplace.

The knowledge and skill base required of our employees will change in response to both technology and the need to produce more with tighter resources. A somewhat smaller workforce, with a changing composition, will be called upon to keep the machinery of our economy moving. This will present a frustrating challenge for business owners and managers as they compete for people that will have to be trained to perform the tasks asked of them.

A new generation of college graduates with teaching degrees will find jobs in industry, teaching basic literacy skills to high school graduates who lack the knowledge to meet minimal requirements. Companies will have to provide this educational support to bridge the gap in employee availability. They'll have to grow their own "good people."

Attitudes

Attitudes will regain their importance in the workplace and in other aspects of our lives. Attitudes will spell the difference between "good" employees and also-rans. Employers will offer attitude training in an effort to help marginal employees become the kind of workers that will be needed to meet increasing competitive challenges.

The attitude training will make a difference for many employees, as they discover more of their real potential. For others, it just won't work. It will be too difficult for them to overcome the counterproductive attitudes learned so well over the years. Some of these folks will wonder ignorantly why the world is passing them by.

Those employees with the right "stuff" will be highly successful, enjoying rewarding and satisfying careers. The demand for such people will practically assure them fulfillment in their chosen endeavors. They will have a wide range of exciting opportunities to join the teams of people working for different employers. The 1990s will be active years for executive recruitment firms, with similar high levels of activity among "headhunters" searching for available non-executive talent.

Leadership

Managers will adopt and apply *leadership* skills in the workplace. The old hard-line management techniques, the autocratic approach, simply won't work in most environments. There is no question that participative management is here to stay.

Unfortunately, precious few people in management positions today really know how to be leaders. A whole new set of skills will have to be learned and practiced to enable people and organizations to excel. Colleges and universities will add more human relations classes to their offerings in response to the need in the marketplace.

Organizations of all kinds will provide remedial and skill-sharpening training and development, focused on helping their managers and executives understand how to work more effectively with people. This training will focus on team leadership, sales, and customer service.

Sales and Service

Selling goods and services will become more consumer oriented. Sales will be made on the basis of long-standing relationships in which professional sales counselors help customers buy what is best for them. Service after the sale will become increasingly important for salespeople in all fields as competition strains to earn the right to modify buying patterns. Salespeople who become proficient in this changing style will be in high demand.

Customer service will become an integral part of corporate strategy. The concept will extend far beyond "smile training" and slogans. Consumers at organizational and personal levels will expect higher quality in both merchandise and service. A resurgence of consumerism will emphasize service, providing wonderful opportunities in the growing field of customer service for people-oriented employees.

Roles and Structure

To get the jobs done, people on the front lines will be expected to accept greater responsibility. Accountability, along with increased authority, will extend beyond senior management levels right down to the hourly employees. We will expect more from those "on the ground floor" of our organizations as companies thin their management ranks.

Corporate structures will change as middle managers are replaced with computers and other technological tools. More people who now hold management titles will become functional specialists, providing support to fellow team members. An enhanced sense of cooperation will displace the fiefdoms that many staff and line departments have become.

Employees will have more freedom in determining how their work will be done. The emphasis will be on results and collaboration, rather than on activities and departmental independence. The trend toward managers having the choice of purchasing needed resources in-house or from outside vendors will continue. Leadership, relationships, quality, and service will become key ingredients for survival.

While good people will be hard for some employers to attract, others will have their pick. The difference will be in the hiring company's reputation. Issues of concern in that reputation will be how people work together, opportunities to make a difference (which means a significant degree of control over one's destiny), corporate responsibility to employees and to society, meaningful work with growth potential, and both intrinsic and extrinsic rewards.

Changing for the Future

The changes will be comfortable for some organizations, painful for others. Some employers are already well on their way, operating to a significant extent according to the strategies presented in this book. Unfortunately, some companies will not change. Many are already having difficulties. Most of the inflexible organizations will disappear.

The 1990s and beyond will be exciting times. The employers who attract and keep their good people will become magnets for more high quality employees. Working together with a common vision and dedicated leadership, these teams of conscientious people will enjoy being on the leading edge...on the competitive edge.

Eventually, other elements of society will follow the pattern. We'll see a gradual improvement of standards and performance in all sectors of our economy. A trend of increasing acceptance of responsibility and accountability will strengthen our educational system, the management of our environment, and a whole host of other aspects of our lives.

We're on the threshold of a resurgence! Each of us has the potential to enjoy the thrill of riding the wave successfully into the next century. The knowledge we need is already here. We know what we need to do to keep people productive and part of our team.

The future belongs to those who *do* what needs to be done.

Keeping Good People

APPENDICES

Appendix A

Behavioral Styles, Leadership Styles

For generations people mused about what made people "tick." Why did some people behave one way, while other people behaved differently under the same circumstances?

In the late 1890s, Karl Jung suggested that human behavior can be classified in different categories, or types. He became known as the Father of Type Psychology. His work was very helpful in understanding behavior.

In 1928, Dr. William Marston published *Emotions Of Normal People*. In a pioneering move, Marston mapped human behavior in four quadrants on a two-axis system. One axis measured direct versus indirect approach, while the other addressed people orientation versus task orientation. This was the seminal research for most of the study on needs-generated behavior that has been done since.

A number of psychological tests and learning instruments have been developed over the years to help us understand and use the four-quadrant behavioral knowledge. A leader in the field of these materials is the Personal Profile System developed by Dr. John Geier.

The four primary behavioral styles, as shown in the Personal Profile and associated instruments are *dominant*, *influencer* or *interacting*, *steadfast*, and *compliance* or *cautious*.

Using the initials of the descriptors, the styles and the framework have become known as the "DiSC" approach.

Each of the styles is different from the others. Each is unique, with its own strengths. Each style of behavior, and each of us, is motivated by different needs. Our behavior is unique, individually and in groups. No style can be characterized as being "better" than another.

The more we can understand about human behavior, the more effective we can be in managing ourselves and in working with others. The more you understand and appreciate others, and what motivates them, the better you can work with them in a team environment, the better you can meet their needs, and the better chance you have of keeping them.

Before we look at the four primary styles of behavior, it's important to note that only about 15% of the population is recognized as a "pure type" Dominant, Influencer, Steadfast, or Cautious. Research shows that about 85% of us are some mixture of the four primary styles, possessing the needs and outward behaviors of more than one of the primary styles.

Most of us use one of the styles as our primary behavior, with a second style as a secondary, or back-up, behavior. The more you can learn about how the styles interact, the stronger you will be in working with others.

Dominant

The first primary style we'll discuss is the Dominant type. Dominant people are characteristically determined and results-oriented. They can be demanding and directive as they exercise their tendency to take charge. Dominant people are risk-takers and innovators who enjoy challenges. They like variety in their lives, with the power and authority to get things done.

Freedom from controls and supervision is important for Dominant behavior types, as they seek a wide scope of operations. They like to get things done, to show their accomplishments. Dominants like quick, direct answers.

Careful analysis and weighing of pros and cons is not characteristic of this style, and social graces may appear to be comparable to the proverbial bull in the china shop.

Influencer

These folks are people-oriented. They love being with other people and are usually gregarious. They're positive, enthusiastic, and persuasive. Great talkers, Influencers enjoy entertaining people and helping others. You may see them as emotional and impulsive as they exercise their freedom of expression.

Influencers want freedom from outside controls and from the details of their work. They prefer to be the motivators, the initiators, the people who come up with great ideas and inspire others to follow them to fulfill those dreams. It is not characteristic of this style to concentrate on facts or task completion, to be well organized, or to be highly objective in decision making.

Steadfast

Our third behavior style is characterized by a high concern for getting tasks accomplished in a systematic, predictable pattern. They like security and stability and are seen as being very patient, loyal, and supportive. Steadfast people are usually very good listeners, adept at solving problems in a deliberate and caring manner.

Specialists in their areas of endeavor, they appreciate sincere expressions of appreciation for their work. Their preference is to work with established procedures and guidelines, without abrupt changes. When change does have to occur, they are more supportive if they have input and if the changes are well-planned before implementation.

Cautious

People exhibiting the fourth style of behavior are highly oriented toward control, standard operating procedures, rules and regulations, and quality assurance. They are concerned with accuracy, details, critical thinking to research and analyze, and careful deliberation. Cautious people are usually diplomatic, but practically insist on compliance to recognized standards.

Anxious to see things done the right way, Cautious people are firm in their beliefs and rather set in their ways. They resist change--if it's worked well for 20 years, why change it?. They prefer a sheltered environment and reassurances to being on the cutting edge of development where risk and creativity is the byword.

With a deeper understanding of the needs-oriented behavior of yourself and your people, you can do a much more effective job of leadership. Included in this behavioral knowledge is an appreciation of the goals and the fears of each style:

Primary Behavioral Style	Goal	Fear
dominant	directness	being taken advantage of
influencer	social recognition	social rejection
steadfast	traditional practices	loss of stability
cautious	proper way, self,discipline	criticism of work effort

Team effectiveness is dependent on the way people work with each other. Each person is motivated by his/her own needs, and brings that orientation to the team. Based on its composition, the team could be well-balanced in terms of the representation of the various styles. If there are too many of one style and too few of another, relatively speaking, the team could be out of balance and therefore less effective.

Supervisors and managers, in their leadership role, can achieve much higher levels of productivity, teamwork, satisfaction, and stability if they are attentive to the significance of the behavioral styles. People relate differently to each other based on their style and perspective. Leaders who understand their style and the style of each of their team members can be more attentive to meeting individual needs.

People with different behavioral styles approach conflict differently. Part of the leader's job is to resolve conflicts quickly and in ways that will be acceptable to all parties.

People will tend to remain as employees where their individuality is respected and appreciated. Much of this understanding and insight into how to deal with people flows from gaining and applying knowledge of behavioral styles.

These behavioral styles have been presented at a basic level to provide readers with a quick working knowledge and appreciation of the various approaches people have to their environments. Further information, learning instruments, and tools for analysis and application of behavioral knowledge are available from:

Herman Associates, Inc.
19 North Main Street
Rittman, Ohio 44270-1407
(216) 927-3566.

Leadership Styles

Quite a few studies have been done of leadership styles over the years. A number of helpful theories provide insight and understanding of the various perspectives on leadership. These theories are valuable information for managers to learn, since keeping good people often depends on using the right leadership style for the situation.

Your local library will be a good source of information for those interested in gaining further knowledge on this topic. Management and leadership textbooks provide good explanations of the various theories and their application. College and university libraries will also be good resources.

Several of the more familiar theories are the situational leadership model developed by Paul Hersey and Kenneth Blanchard, the managerial grid developed by Robert Blake and Jane Mouton, and Theory X/Theory Y developed by Douglas McGregor.

In its own way, each of these theories looks at how leaders perform with the degree of attention they give to task or directive behavior versus people or supportive behavior. Each has a different way of describing the varying styles. There are, of course, positive and negative consequences of pursuing any leadership style, depending on your perspective.

One point of emphasis prevalent today is to remain flexible and responsive to your people. Leadership practices must be individualized; the way you work with one person may not be as effective with another member of your team. Your challenge as a leader is to provide the appropriate kind of leadership for each of your people so they can each do their best, as individual performers and as members of work teams and of the entire organization.

This is not easy to do, especially for managers who have not been schooled in the fine art of leadership. This is an important area for training and development of managers. To be effective leaders able to keep good people and keep everyone highly productive in the 1990s and beyond, managers at all levels in all kinds of organizations must learn how to lead.

Supervisors lead team members at the operational level of the organization. Their need is to understand technical skills first, to be able to answer questions from subordinates. Second, they must develop a strong understanding of people and how to work with them. Supervisors get things done through other people, so the relationships have to be positive and productive.

Middle managers also need well-honed people skills, but are expected to perform with more of a conceptual orientation than technical. People at this level should be more concerned with the allocation of resources to accomplish the organization's goals and objectives. Procedures, systems, and interpretation of policies are part of their role.

Senior managers of organizations will be stronger with technical and conceptual skills, their focus must be on the corporate mission, development and review of policies, and long-range planning. People skills continue to have importance, since most of what senior managers do involves heavy interpersonal communication.

People want to excel in their work. They want their organization to excel. To make this possible, the entire management team must lead with consistency and cohesiveness. No longer can we point the finger of blame at labor; the problem is with management.

The opportunity for high achievement rests with management. If managers, as leaders, perform well for their employing organization, non-managerial employees will gladly follow them. If they are understood, appreciated, and treated appropriately, many good people will be happy to stay with one team for a long period of time.

Satisfaction, and resultant high productivity and stability, come from the way you work with the various kinds of people on your team, applying the right kind of leadership techniques to get things done.

Appendix B

Personal and Organizational Values

In previous chapters of this book, we examined one (of two) major internal motivators of human behavior. Thus far, you have been provided with an overview of how "needs" drive affects behavior and performance. In Chapter 4, you read about the various need types or levels. Appendix A described behavior determined by needs. These behavioral styles determine *how* we pursue the satisfaction of the various need levels.

Our values or beliefs make up the second major internal (or individual) motivator. Values are defined as the standards or principles we use to guide our decisions and actions.

There is a direct connection or relationship between an individual's needs and that person's values or beliefs. Both of these internal drives shape one's performance.

Let's examine the relationship between needs and values first, then we will discuss the other life forces which initially and continually develop our values perspectives or belief positions.

Group I needs levels (physiological or survival and safety or security) tend to be accompanied by a values perspective which is *self*-oriented.

Group II needs levels (social and other esteem) are accompanied by an *other*-oriented perspective. Others provide the direction for the behavior or the decisions.

Group III needs levels (self esteem and self-actualization) are generally accompanied by a perspective which places value on *integrating* self, others, and society.

Of course, the picture is not that simple. In addition to needs, other forces shape our values. Original parenting shapes children's values. However, if parenting does not meet a child's emotional, psychological, or physical safety needs, parental values programming is generally not successful.

Values are also shaped by schools, churches, media, and what's going on societally or culturally. Values shaping is also a function of demographics such as geographic location as well as the family's economic standing. Peers play an important role in the values-shaping process for young people.

The teenage years present a clear example of the relationship between needs and values. The young person is generally motivated by needs-generated social concerns. Physiological and security needs are largely taken care of by the parents.

Social needs and the related other-oriented valued perspectives are frequently evident in behavior which is group (peer) driven. Other influences, peer pressure, and peer acceptance motivate such teen behavior.

A major milestone in the continuing development of personal values is the acceptance of responsibility. Generally, this occurs right after the teenage period, which is primarily focused on self and others' rights. Significant life experiences, life crises, change in roles, institutional forces or any combination will bring about this change in perspective.

Let's use an example for a deeper examination of the relationship between needs and values. Paul, 27, and employee in your organization, is very responsibility- oriented. He is a good team player, loyal to his work group. He works hard. He values the respect of his peers and his manager. His day-to-day behavior and his decisions reflect these values. He comes in early and works late, as the workload dictates. These behaviors are not demanded by his superior; they are a result of Paul's own internal motivation.

Paul's apartment lease is not renewed. Apartment rentals have climbed steeply since he moved in several years ago. Then

Paul's car is stolen. Insurance proceeds will not cover the purchase of a new or decent used automobile.

At this point, safety and security needs take on increasing importance for Paul. His behavior reflects increasing self orientation. He may even raise a "what's-in-it-for-me" question when the team is assigned a project which will require extra work effort and time. Previously, his team orientation would have motivated him, without financial reward. Now, however, Paul is more needs-motivated.

Does that mean that the responsibility orientation to the team is gone? Has Paul ceased to value the respect of his peers or his manager? Of course not!

Yet, his behavior may be much more self-oriented until his safety and security needs are once more satisfied.

There is an ongoing interaction between needs and values regardless of the needs level or the values orientation.

In another phase of values development, self-respect, responsibility to (and for) self become uppermost. The individual values integrating self with others, groups, and society. Responsibility at this phase is not to, or for, others. Responsibility is not to the rules of the group, team, organization, or traditional group.

Rather, responsibility is to examine the situation and determine the best course of action for *all* concerned. Therefore, a person motivated by this values perspective is more questioning than accepting. An individual with this values perspective does not value rules necessarily as *the* guides for decisions or actions. Rather, the individual values taking responsibility to personally think through the situation and, subsequently, decide upon the most appropriate decision for all concerned. Responsibility of this decision-making process is accepted by the individual. The individual also recognizes that accountability and responsibility go hand-in-hand.

This values perspective generally accompanies the individual who is motivated by self esteem and self-actualization needs.

Organizational Values

Now, what does this all mean to organizations? Like individuals, organizations are needs-motivated. In fact, survival needs are most predominant in a young company. Safety and security needs, needs to establish financial stability, are met next. It is not until these are satisfied that the employer, or the employee, will be interested in social, procedural, structural, and developmental needs.

An organization's values are usually those held by the social forces. A company's founder established its original operational values. The way employees and customers are valued, the basic assumptions which guide and structure a company, are a direct reflection of the original founder and the company's continuing social forces.

Too frequently, the values which are to guide individual, much less organizational behavior, have never been identified nor clarified. An organizational mission, or purpose, that exceeds mere needs motivation, is never developed. Or worse yet, a philosophy is espoused, but the actions of the organization are not congruent with the espoused philosophy.

Together, the organization's needs and values make up its norms. Norms are the written (or unwritten) rules, behavioral expectations, policies, and procedures (formal as well as informal). Individual performance and behavior that adapts to these norms usually meets with organizational approval and reward. Behavior which does not fit with the norms is not successful.

Organizational norms built merely upon needs motivation can not long or satisfactorily guide or motivate employee behavior. An organization's culture and norms must include the values which create an environment motivational to its employees. Without clear and identified values, it is impossible to build this motivational culture or develop these organizational norms.

Let's consider another specific example. In today's competitive business environment, customer service is frequently an organization's only competitive edge. Quality is no longer motivational for purchasing. It is simply expected. Quality does not attract customers. *Poor* quality, however, does cause an organization to lose customers. Price, another past competitive edge, is a competitive advantage no longer. The costs of products and services are generally quite similar. Service, then, is the value-added element which still creates the edge over one's competition.

Now, let's look at customer service that is driven by needs motivation alone. The motivation for customer service does not come from customer or employee values. The objective is solely dollar income.

It is not long before employees who are aware catch on. They are not valued. Policies, procedures, and the corporate structure do not reveal any real values for relationships with either customers or employees. Employees are not accorded the same treatment that they are expected (by norm expectations) to show the customer. All too soon, the customer catches on. It is difficult for an employee to treat customers with courtesy and respect when they, themselves, are given none.

Some organizations monitor customer service department telephone calls. What is the underlying assumption? What is the belief system that underlies this assumption? Clearly, the belief system is that employees are unwilling or unable to perform. They are not worthy of trust, certainly. Otherwise, their calls would not be monitored. Now, can you imagine employees whose organization is clearly expecting untrustworthiness, incompetence, unwillingness to not provide the expected behavior? Clearly, such an organization has never heard of expectation theory.

Only with a clear organizational mission/purpose built upon needs *and* values can a clearly recognizable culture be developed. Clearly articulated mission or purpose statements can communicate to one and all what the organization stands for.

In the selection and hiring process, such clarity is invaluable. Turnover is extremely expensive, particularly at upper management levels. Yet, it is at these very levels that organizational and individual values become increasingly important and evident.

If you intend to *keep* good people, it is imperative that the organization's values be clear, be communicated well, and be reflected in decisions, norms, structures, policies, and procedures. Values conflicts between employees and the organization cause conflict, frustration, and decline in productivity. The best employees will leave, rather than remain in such a situation.

Define what you believe in, and what your organization believes in. Share those beliefs with your people so there is a clear understanding of what is expected. If the values culture is strong enough, those who don't fit will leave quite willingly, often before you have an opportunity to make such a suggestion.

Appendix C

Self Esteem in the Corporate Environment

An increasing number of people are becoming interested in self esteem. The concept, and the term, is becoming popularized with our sharpening focus on the value of the individual.

Numerous consultants, authors, trainers, and professional speakers spread the word about self esteem. They approach it from a number of perspectives. Many of these exponents of self esteem seek to motivate their audiences; others look for holistic approaches to the good life.

A recognized national leader in the self esteem field is William J. McGrane, CPAE. Bill has devoted much of his adult life to the study of the topic and its practical application in life. Director of The McGrane Self Esteem Institute in Cincinnati, Ohio, Bill talks enthusiastically about how we can build human self esteem in organizational settings.

I am familiar with Bill's philosophies, and I admire and respect his approach, depth, and sincerity. To give you some insight into self esteem and its place in the corporate world, I interviewed Bill. The balance of this appendix will be a sharing of his comments.

Rather than burden you with the confusion of questions, answers, and commentary, I will quote or paraphrase Bill so you can experience his thoughts directly.

Let's begin with the premise that all human beings have been born with the birthright and the gift of high self esteem.

It is present within all of us, although many people have buried it away from their consciousness.

We seem to lose our awareness of our self esteem over the years as we learn to value other measures of personal worth. As we shift our attention from genuine self esteem, we tend to hurt and be hurt more easily. We don't have the inner resilience we need; we become more fragile.

As we realize we're missing something, we begin searching. We don't know quite what we're looking for, but we know there must be something more. In our materialistic society, we usually get caught up in the concern for self image. It's a stage we go through and, unfortunately, many of us never quite come out of it.

Self image is *different* than self esteem. Self image is comparison. If you run your company to compare one employee with the next, you are setting yourself up to lose employees. Self esteem says I am valuable just because I exist. It's a self respect that I feel for myself; it has nothing to do with what I do or what I have.

That's tough for people to accept as reality. God set it up that way. He doesn't say you have to have anything or do anything to be loved by Him. Self esteem is feared by a lot of people because it forces you to look inside. And that's difficult. People need to recognize that each of us has a uniqueness. When we value others because of their uniqueness, they will be encouraged to develop their competence and their self esteem.

As we go through life, all of us make unwise choices. Our objective, as we grow and learn and strengthen our self esteem, is to make fewer and fewer unwise choices. Once we realize this, we become internally motivated to rebuild our self esteem. That exciting process is achieved through three steps.

To raise your self esteem, you
1. review your personal history
2. re-program personal history as a result of the discoveries we make through unwise behavior

3. take action.

Your level of self esteem is based on what you *do* after you've learned more about yourself. Your sense of personal worth actually comes from what you do for others, more than what you do for yourself. High self esteem comes most to those who give of themselves to serve others, without any concern for reward or return. It's what I call personal tithing of one's talents.

True wealth comes from unselfish service. The concept of supporting others, of helping others grow and prosper, is a manifestation of genuine self esteem. The manager who invests energy in supporting others, helping them realize their potential, is building his/her own self esteem while enabling other people to build theirs.

Let's look at what happens in the corporate environment. In reality, we are able to keep people in a job even when the financial rewards may not be as high as the psychic rewards. In a money-oriented society, we wonder how this can happen.

To understand how self esteem is applied wisely in organizations, let's look at the concept of bonding. I believe that the first year and half a human being is alive, the most precious gift we can give is the gift of bonding.

When bonding occurs, the child feels safe, secure, and comfortable. Those three words are critical if you're going to create an environment where people can thrive in an atmosphere of cooperation and trust.

Enlightened parents will leave the furniture where it is for at least the first three years so the child will sense stability and security. The child can count on being safe, secure, and comfortable every single day. A frightening number of children today miss this vital bonding because both parents are working.

With both parents working, the child does not get the bonding because the parents need to work for family survival. Companies on the cutting edge could set aside a sufficient amount of space and create a day care center inside the company.

Such a facility on the company premises, would allow for more bonding between parent and child. The parent can be with the child during lunch and perhaps during breaks. This provides the child with a greater sense of continuity. The bonding deepens every day, but doesn't interfere with the flow of work or the continuity within the company. The parent forms a stronger bond with the company as a result of the company's support for the family bonding.

Unfortunately, this is not being done to any great extent in companies today. I believe it is part of our future, and caring employers should prepare to offer the service. There is a wonderful opportunity to support people, to hold good people, and to increase the psychic rewards.

Psychic rewards account for 95% of our desired income. Only 5% of our personal needs come as a result of financial reward. We have proven this ratio, and our news reports are full of stories validating this balance.

Psychic rewards recognize people for who they are, not for what they do. We are a society that values people for what they do and what they have. Yet, greed, power, and money have not brought fulfillment to people. Today we see this more and more, causing people to look for that elusive "something else."

The high self esteem, value-driven, companies that will be most successful in the 1990s and beyond will be those organizations that model the behavior they want their employees to show themselves. This means our corporate leaders need to have high self esteem, personally and organizationally. If I don't hold a certain feeling myself, there's no way I can model that feeling to someone else.

Therefore, companies need to hire and manage people based on clear understandings of ethics, company policies, legitimate job descriptions, and vital job functions. These have to be reviewed constantly and re-affirmed. The people being led need to have considerable input into how their jobs are structured and how they are being measured.

Evaluations need to be done at the time of performance, not six months later. The "sandwich" approach to discipline is, quite frankly, outmoded and obsolete. Evaluations need to be given as *affirmations*, emphasizing the positive aspects and looking at how other aspects might be improved.

The manager needs to accept the reality of the employee's existing skills, with a willingness to let the employee refine and strengthen those skills that need work. Note that the responsibility to improve is on the *employee*. Self esteem is built by allowing people to take more responsibility for themselves.

Ideally, the employer would allocate a significant sum of money for each employee to invest in self-development each year. The employee would be trusted to select those learning experiences. The employee would have the freedom to make the choices about which learning they want to take place in their lives.

The growing employee would have the responsibility of gaining worthwhile knowledge, then sharing it with others. If you're going to have an atmosphere of trust, you'd better let the employee make the choices. Based on the choices the employee makes from year to year, the manager may be involved very little in structuring the learning.

I believe the more freedom you give to employees, the longer you are going to keep the employees. They feel needed, wanted, important, and valued. These are all basic areas of raising people's self esteem. Unless people are affirmed daily, we're kidding ourselves. Few people get affirmed daily in any part of this country or part of the world. I'm very firm about this.

Keeping good people does not take large amounts of money. It takes a personal investment. The organization's leaders, including the CEO, need to be visible to their people. The less visible they are, the more they set themselves up for high turnover. Bonding, being with their people, needs to be their Number One issue daily. People need to be affirmed daily.

Unfortunately, many people in senior management positions are from the "old school" that doesn't place such an importance on caring for the individual. When men dominated the workplace, things were different. They didn't experience strong bonding, as a rule, when they were children. So, they don't use bonding at work. It simply isn't there.

Today, and on into the future, we will see how having more women in the workplace increases this concern for bonding. I believe that men are more concerned about things; women are more concerned about relationships. Both men and women need to be sensitive to this perspective and find the right balance. We can be highly productive with strong concern for each other, with bonding, with relationships.

You motivate people by valuing them. To the degree you value them, they will not steal, they will not manipulate, they'll act as if they own the company. It's good for employees to have some real personal ownership in the company. To the extent possible, particularly in public corporations, give employees the opportunity to buy stock in the company...to own a little piece.

When people buy into the organization, they have a higher level of commitment. Now they're concerned about the character of the company as a whole, in addition to their own character.

People perform better if character is encouraged, versus personality. The character of an individual, when developed, will be a high self esteem or low self esteem. The character of the business will be determined by how employees act. If you act as if you own the company, keeping the concerns of others and of the whole above concerns for yourself, your people will follow your lead.

"Intimacy" will be a byword of the 1990s, even though it still makes men uncomfortable. Paraphrasing, it could easily read, "into me see." To the degree that you see into me, to the degree you know me as a person, to the degree that you invest time with me as a person, you and I will have a relationship that is based on more than just business.

Take time to get to know your employees, and help them get to know you. Focus on the person, the family, outside interests, ideas, creativity, and similar concerns. Learn to value each other as human beings, not just as parts of the business.

I recommend people take 15-minute segments on some sort of regular basis to get to know each other. Character, self esteem, relationships, are built through bonding. Managers need to invest the time to open up *as people* with their employees to establish and maintain long-term, mutually beneficial, relationships that are intimate...based on the level of intimacy that each person can have.

When people invest in this sharing, this knowing each other, this intimacy, in business organizations, the resultant relationships will produce a level of productivity beyond their wildest dreams.

You can't stop this process. You can't just do it one year and that's it. It's deliberate, daily, constant affirmations that reinforce the belief system. Put your principles up on the wall for everyone to see them. Talk about them daily. Become more principle-directed, rather than need-directed.

Help people understand, by your talking about your principles and acting according to your principles, what you stand for. As an example, can you say "no" to cheating somebody? Can you say "no" to stealing from somebody? Can you say "no" when somebody undercharges you? Can you say "no" when something simply isn't right?

When you direct your energies to helping others, to building character, you become much more powerful than if you are just helping yourself. Self esteem is considerably higher when we concentrate on serving others instead of serving ourselves. We feel better about what we are doing. We feel better about the organization we do it with. We *bond* with that organization because of the compatibility of our character.

That bonding, that reinforcement of self esteem, holds people in the company. That bonding produces a feeling of being safe, secure, and comfortable. When people gain that feeling, they don't want to risk losing it by leaving the company to go somewhere else. They'll stay where they are valued for who they are.

People want to like where they work. They don't want to have a *thank-God-it's-Friday* attitude. They want to work where they have friends, where there are others who want to help the work become satisfying and fulfilling. They want to help the company be successful, so they can be successful, too.

People don't leave companies because of money, because of how much they got paid or didn't get paid. They leave because they didn't feel they were valuable, important, or needed enough. Once you know you're needed, you'll stay in that environment. Psychic income will always overpower money, even though people may say that's not true.

If a company pays me and rewards me for my productivity, both psychically and financially, then I will stay there. There's no need for me to move elsewhere where I don't know what the atmosphere is going to be like. I have what I want and need here. Bonding.

People would rather remain where they have bonded, escalating those bonds, than take the risk of going somewhere else where they may not have those feelings. Value people for who they are, and they will stay with you...happy and productive.

Keeping Good People

INDEX

INDEX

A

Aburdene, Patricia, 45
accessibility, 154
accountabilities, define, 179
achievements, celebration of, 86
advancement opportunities, 91
appreciation, 131, 253
appreciation, of routine work, 196
approval, 188
associations, trade and
professional, 222
atmospheric conditions, 108
attitudes, 19
attracting good people, 24
authority, define, 180
awareness of what people do, 187

B

barriers to accomplishment, 170
behavioral styles, 111
benefits, flexible, 211
birthdays, celebration of, 86
Blake, Robert, 261
Blanchard, Kenneth, 260
bonding, 281
boredom, 198
breaks, 199
break times, freedom, 100
business plan, use of, 97

C

camaraderie, 76
care about people, 153
career development drive, 9
cautious behavioral style, 259
celebrations, 86
challenges, 167, 216
child care services, 106
clarity of policies, 89
color, in decoration, 108
comfort zone in careers, 249
commercial seminars, 220
commitment to people, 94
common vision, 60
communication, 117
communications systems, 105
compensation, show value of, 203
compensation, flexible, 211
compensation, leverage of, 206
compensation, skills-based, 206
competency building, 230
competition for good people, 22
compliance behavior style, 259
complaints, response to, 96
confidence, 146
conflict resolution, 113
contracts, performance, 197
corporate image, 27
corporate values, 273
creativity, inspire, 184

criticism, avoidance of, 176
criticism, balance with praise, 142
customer focus, 67

D

design of reward system, 207
design of tasks, 198
direction, clarity of, 189
discipline, progressive, 83
discrimination, 13, 71
dominant behavior style, 258
dress, freedom of, 100

E

education, support of, 217
employee selection, 100
employee stock ownership, 213
empowerment, personal. 252
empowerment, team, 172
enthusiasm, 66
environment, healthy, safe, 77
environment, safety/security, 109
equipment, 106
ESOPs and employee stock
    ownership, 213
ethics, 59
example, 158
exit interviews, 88

F

failure, permission, 93
fair, 73, 163
family feeling, 74
feedback, specifics in, 200
firm, 163
flexibility, 128
flexibility in working hours, 81
freedom, 128
freedom of choice, 100
frustration, 168
fun, 85

G

Geier, John, 257
good people, defined, 3
gossip, 144
growth, into bigger jobs, 224
growth, intellectual, 227
guidance, 188
Guiding Principles, 69

H

healthy working environment, 77
Hersey, Paul, 260
high potential/low skill
    compensation, 210
honesty, 73
humiliation, avoidance of, 176
humor, 156

I

ideas, welcome new, 176
identity, 104, 139
immigration factor, 17
incentives for growth, 231
incentives, in compensation, 204
individual, value of, 63
individualism, 153, 243
influencer behavioral style, 259
information sharing, 63
initiative, 181
innovation, inspire, 184
insufficient supply of people, 13
integrity, 76
intellectual growth, 227
interacting behavioral style, 259
interviews, exit, 88
involvement, 190
involvement, reward system for, 207

J

job adjustment, 171

job satisfaction, 250
Jung, Karl, 257

K

knowledge deficiency, 14

L

leadership, 159
leadership style, 260
learning materials, 218
learning materials, sources, 219
leverage of cash compensation, 206
limits, establishment, 186
listening, 136
location of company, 102
low skill/high potential
    compensation, 210
loyalty, 65

M

managers set the course, 52
managerial grid, 261
Marston, William, 257
McGregor, Douglas, 261
McGrane, William J., 279
meetings, regular, 114
meetings, spontaneous, 115
Mickey Mouse, 173
motivating factors survey, 43, 46
Mouton, Jane, 261

N

Naisbitt, John, 45
needs, individual, 249
"new woman", 122

O

opportunities for advancement, 91
organizational values, 276
overtime scheduling, 194

P

Pascarella, Perry, 45
parking policy, 105
partners: of education, business, 15
patience, 125
people, factor in competition, 31
people, prime resource, 94
people, value of, 96
performance, feedback on, 200
performance, reward link, 205
performance contracts, 197
permission to fail or succeed, 93
Personal Profile System, 257
personal values, 271
physical strategies, 101
plan, use of business, 97
policies, clear, 89
policies, uniform administration, 91
positives, not negatives, 145
praise, balance with criticism, 142
principles, guiding, 69
profanity, 72
professional standing, value of, 75
progressive discipline, 83
projects, for growth, 229
promises, 174
promote from within, 91

R

real work to do, 165
recognition, 120
refreshments at work station, 99
rejection, avoidance of, 176
reporting, reduce, 191
respect, 126
response to complaints, 96
resources to get job done, 174
responsibilities, challenging, 216
responsibilities, define, 178
responsiveness, 188
restlessness, 254

rewards, for performance, 205
reward system, design, 207
risk in work environment, 70
routine work, appreciation of, 196
rules, avoid stupid, 80

S

safety in workplace, 79
satisfaction, job, 250
school-sponsored seminars, 221
second-guessing, 162
security in work environment, 70
selection of employees, 100
self esteem, 43, 279
seminars, outside, 220
shortage of good people, 11
situational leadership, 260
skills-based compensation, 210
skills gap, 18
solutions to complaints, 96
"special employees", 124
specifics in feedback, 200
stability in work environment, 70
steadfast behavioral style, 259
strategic leadership, 53
stress, 160
stupid rules, avoidance of, 80
supply of good people, 13
support for people, 119

T

talent, discovery of, 226
talk with people, 140
team, work as, 63
Theory X, Theory Y, 261
togetherness, 150
training, learner teach others, 223
trapped in jobs, 10
trust, 130, 193

U

unsuitable people, tolerance, 87

V

vacations, scheduling, 100
values, personal and corporate, 273
values and ethical standards, 112
value each individual, 63
vision, share common, 60

W

work, make it fun, 85
work areas, personalization, 104
work together as team, 63
working hours, flexibility, 81
workplace, healthy, 77
workplace safety, 79

Notes

Notes

Notes

Notes

Notes

Notes